FAMILY PRIDE

Also by Donna Beasley

The Family Reunion Planner

DONNA BEASLEY

FAMILY PRIDE

THE COMPLETE GUIDE TO TRACING
AFRICAN-AMERICAN
GENEALOGY

MACMILLAN • USA

Macmillan
A Simon & Schuster Macmillan Company
1633 Broadway
New York, NY 10019

ISBN 0-02-860842-9

Book design by Nick Anderson

Printed in the United States of America

This book is dedicated to my family: my wonderful mother and father, Lindsey and Helen Smith; my terrific brothers, Milton, Charles, and Michael; my nieces and nephews, Michelle, Milton Jr., Brandi, Donnie, Cameo, and Blain; my marvelous and numerous aunts, uncles, and cousins. Thank you for a lifetime of love that fills my heart with family pride.

and

To my ancestors who weathered the storms of history, paved the way for a better future, and passed down our most important family tradition of all, to put God first.

Contents

Foreword

Genealogy research is both an art and a science. Deep inside all of us is the urge to visit, to walk, to commune where our ancestors made their mark. I firmly believe that the recognition of one's self-worth has a direct relationship to the knowledge of his or her history, culture, and family. A family's strong oral tradition as well as the official records of past generations serve as a cornerstone of our search for the past. The specific and generalized information is exciting, informative, and alluring—once started many suggest they are unable to let go. That is what captured the imagination and dedication of my late father, Alex Haley. It is this phenomenon that caused the author Donna Beasley to search for her family's beginnings.

The record of struggle and accomplishment must be preserved and taught to young family members. Reciting the genealogy of a family and the associated storytelling by its elders involves the passing on of values and the concepts of hope and spirituality from generation to generation. It is participatory rather than passive and allows family members to identify and internalize their identification with the family. It is in this spirit that Donna Beasley has written *Family Pride: The Complete Guide to Tracing African-American Genealogy.* This book is your guide to preserving your family's history for the next generation.

William Alexander Haley
President
Haley Family Corporation

Acknowledgments

I want to thank the many institutions that took the time to provide me with a list of their African-American genealogy holdings, making a genealogy researcher's job just a little easier. A special thanks to the institutions whose holdings provided a good deal of the research and resources in this book: the National Archives in Washington, D.C.; the Library of Congress; the National Regional Archives, the Great Lakes Center in Chicago; the Vivian G. Harsh Research Collection of the Woodson Regional Library of the Chicago Public Library; the genealogy collection of the Avalon branch of the Chicago Public Library; the Newberry Library's genealogical collection in Chicago; the Allen County Library's genealogical collection in Fort Wayne, Indiana; the Chicago Historical Society's photography archivists.

A special thanks to Jane Crouse, who helped with the book's editing and motivated me to keep my writing on track and on schedule.

A special thanks to Thelma Strong-Eldridge, researcher, who was a great help in compiling the book's resource section. She is president of the Patricia Liddell Researchers, the Chicago chapter of the African-American Historical and Genealogical Society.

A special thanks to genealogists Roland Barksdale Hall and Jeanette Braxton-Secret, who shared parts of their family's story in this book.

Introduction

Ⴎ

Have you ever had a day that changed your life? Or made a great self-discovery? It happened to me one sunny spring day in Washington, D.C., in 1980. My job with an advertising agency had taken me to the nation's capital on business. I stayed an extra day to visit the National Archives, a library that houses much of our nation's history. Held lovingly in its fireproof vaults are the original parchments of the Declaration of Independence, the U.S. Constitution, and the Bill of Rights. It also contains other historically valuable records of our country's past, such as census reports and military records. It was these latter records that were of interest to me.

I had just begun to research my family's history. The archives were reported to be a must visit for genealogists. As I climbed the marble steps of this massive gray container, I felt butterflies in my stomach. I was excited, probably the way archaeologists feel going on their first dig in a distant land. I was a novice, a student archaeologist you might say, out to dig up my family's history.

I was researching my mother's family, the Gores. She was one of twenty children. At this point, I had done some census research at the branch office of the National Archives in Chicago and a couple of oral interviews. My mother's family came from Harris County, Georgia, so I began with that county's census records of 1910. I loaded the microfilm on the projector, pulled my seat into position, and began the hunt. I could trace my maternal grandfather's family back to 1870 with no problem, but found nothing prior to then. It seemed my family's records disappeared once the Civil War began in 1861. My great-grandparents had been slaves. It was customary for slaves to take the surnames of their owners. However, I couldn't find any Gores who owned land in 1860 or 1850 in Harris County or nearby counties. After spending a couple of hours researching my maternal grandfather's family lineage with no luck, I checked my watch. I still had two hours before I needed to head for the airport, so I decided to spend the remaining time researching my maternal grandmother's family. I didn't know anything about them except their surname was Parker and they also were from Harris County.

I got the 1900 census microfilm for Parkers, reloaded the machine, pulled up my chair, and once again began the hunt. That's when my life changed. That's when I made the great discovery. That's when genealogy went from a temporary short-term research project to a lifelong passion. There, among the census records, the Parker branch of my family's tree began to unfold before me. As I traced my family back in time, it seemed as if my ancestors were reaching out to me to tell their story. A story of joy and pain. History sprang to life as I placed my family in the historical context of time tracing ancestors back to 1790.

I finally understood why the skin coloring of my family went from beige, to cinnamon, to chestnut brown, to dark chocolate. Why our hair color went from sandy, to red, to auburn, to brown, to jet black. I discovered I was black, white, and red; African, Irish, and Cherokee. I also discovered the Parker plantation where my great-grandfather and six of his fifteen sisters and brothers had been slaves. Running out of time I began to scramble, writing feverishly and making microfiche copies. I left late. Luckily a cab was unloading right outside the building. I hopped in and yelled, "Airport, please!" I made a silent prayer for God to "please hold that plane."

Looking back at the gray archive building, I realized the butterflies were all aflutter in my stomach again, this time from the excitement of having found a buried treasure from this most successful hunt. I knew the National Archives were a depository for some of the history of my country. Until that day, however, I never really believed it contained any clues to my family's history. Suddenly I felt connected—to my family, to history, and to my country. I knew I had to know more.

That visit to the archives launched my fifteen-year pursuit of genealogy research. It started as a hobby, grew to a passion, and became a lifelong quest. There is always a lead to follow or another family member to interview. My research has taken me to Chicago, Illinois; Washington, D.C.; Atlanta, Georgia; Harris County, Georgia; and Columbus, Georgia. I've spent countless hours poring over handwritten official records and census reports in archives, libraries, cemeteries, and courthouses of these cities. The highlight of my research was conducting the numerous oral interviews arranged with relatives. Each interview was like opening a historical time capsule, never knowing what I'd find, but always worth the trip.

From that visit to the National Archives in 1981, I discovered a whole line of Parker relatives who had moved to Detroit while the Gores moved to Chicago. Like many black families, mine came North for work in the industrial cities. The auto industry lured the Parkers to Detroit while the steel industry held out hope for the Gores in Chicago.

In 1995, I self-published a book on my findings to share with my family. *Family Pride—The Story of the Parkers and the Gores* spanned from 1790 to 1970. The book is divided into two parts. The first part is the earliest history of my family through the marriage and life of my grandparents. It includes some understanding of our African capture as a people, our slave past, contributions to the Civil War, interracial love, and painful tragedies.

The second part is devoted to my grandparents' twenty children. It is a personal snapshot of the siblings' lives, told in their own voices through oral interviews I conducted from 1980 to 1995. That work led to the opportunity to write this book.

I found solutions to many of the problems African-American genealogists face, such as how to find black ancestors in the Revolutionary War, various ports of entry for slave ships, how to find plantation records of slave masters, and much more. Genealogy research can be a rewarding experience, but it is time-consuming, and requires a personal commitment. Often there is no one to ask for guidance. This book is your guide and will jump-start your search to build your own family tree.

It is my hope that I can encourage you to research your own family's genealogy. Historian John Henrick Clark said, "History is a clock that people use to find themselves on the map of human geography. It tells them where they are, and what they are." I feel family history tells you who you are and to whom you belong. Family history also tells where you've been and provides a basis for understanding both where you are and where you are going.

I think you'll find your family's roots are planted deep in American soil, and your family, like mine and many others, helped make this country great. If nothing else, you'll meet your ancestors, share laughs and tears with relatives, connect to history and, I believe, make a great self-discovery. For through a better understanding of our families we acquire an appreciation for their struggles and successes, and we are personally strength-ened by the journey.

If you've already done the research, then let me encourage you to publish your findings. Share what you've discovered with family and friends. Publishing is the final responsibility of the genealogical researcher. So let's begin. Let me show you how to have a good time on the hunt.

Family Pride

HOW TO BEGIN

Twenty years ago hardly any African-Americans had done it. Then Alex Haley's book *Roots* was produced as a television mini-series and interest in African-American family history soared. Over 130 million people watched that show and interest in genealogy has been a growing phenomenon ever since. Haley proved it could be done, and many set out to duplicate his results. Today, thousands of African-Americans have done it—they have traced their family back in time, breathing life into history. Many have discovered their family's history is America's history. The results have often been incredible, shocking, and amazing.

SURPRISES REVEALED

African-American genealogists have discovered connections to this country's first families, such as Thomas Jefferson and first lady Martha Washington.

Jefferson, a slave owner, had two families—one white and one black. Like many slave owners he reportedly fell in love with a slave, Sally Hemings, and that relationship produced several children. Today the black Jefferson lineage is as solid and strong as the white lineage. I once read the black Jeffersons never get invited to the family reunion but have occasionally crashed it. The Jefferson lineage can also be traced to King Edward III of England.

Shirlee Taylor Haizlip writes about her connection to Martha Washington in a book on her family memoirs titled *The Sweeter the Juice*. Additionally, many blacks can trace their lines to the Mount Vernon home of George and Martha Washington. In 1760 he owned 49 slaves; by 1786 he owned 216 slaves.

Other African-American genealogists have discovered amazing adventurers in their family tree. Two are Charles Jacques Ballard and Iverson Granderson.

Ballard was the first black fighter pilot and served in World War I. He ran away to Europe at about age ten as a stowaway aboard a ship. Eventually, by about age eighteen, he made his way to France. Although Negroes were forbidden to fly planes in the U.S. military, this did not deter Ballard. When war broke out he rushed to volunteer and served with distinction in the French Foreign Legion.

Granderson served in the Union Navy during the Civil War aboard several ships, including the USS *Great Western* and USS *Kickapoo*. He didn't exactly enlist; he was a runaway slave who just jumped on board. He then served with valor throughout the Civil War and was honorably discharged in 1865.

As African-Americans researchers, we are sometimes shocked by what we discover. Lynchings, beatings, slave sales, the destruction of slave families, and sharecroppers who were robbed and cheated are often part of our heritage. But that's what so exciting about genealogy. You just don't know who you're going to find on your family tree and what you're going to discover about your family. Understanding what has influenced and shaped your family from a political, social, or economic viewpoint is the direct route to making history live.

LEARNING FROM OTHERS

Most African-Americans who began their genealogy quest fifteen to twenty years ago had little knowledge, experience, and idea of what problems and challenges they were facing. I was among this group of fledgling genealogists. Many of us have honed our detecting skills and solved numerous problems unique to African-American genealogy research over the past two decades. This book will provide both novice and experienced genealogists an opportunity to learn firsthand what problem-solving techniques have worked for others.

HOW SLAVERY AFFECTS YOUR GENEALOGY

African-American genealogy is unique because of the institution of slavery, the common link in the chain of our past. Slaves were forbidden to learn to read or write. Therefore, few written records exist from slaves during that tragic period of America's past. Additionally, during the time of slavery, white masters often had sexual liaisons with black slaves. As a result, there are few African-Americans today that don't have a white ancestor in their family tree. This can be either a curse or a blessing from a genealogical standpoint depending on how records were kept.

Another unique aspect of black genealogy is that slaves were only given first names and commonly used their master's surnames. At the end of slavery, many dropped their master's name and selected another—perhaps dropping the name of a cruel master for that of a previous, kinder master.

Most people know about the slaves and former slaves who served as Union soldiers in all-Negro troops during the Civil War. Few people realize, however, that thousands of slaves also served the Confederacy. Records on black Union soldiers in the Civil War are available at the National Archives and in some libraries. These soldiers and sailors fought valiantly. There are, however, few records on the thousands of freedmen and slaves who were pressed into duty on behalf of both the Union (before the creation of black units) and the Confederacy. Payment for a slave's services was given to the slave owner, not the slave. These men built the bridges and entrenchments, prepared meals, served as blacksmiths, and were the chief grave diggers assigned to burying the 500,000 people who died in the Civil War.

How Far Back Can You Go?

Trying to trace one's ancestry to a particular African village is the toughest challenge we face, and is often an impossible task. However, for about 10 percent of African-Americans it can be done. The key is determining what level of information will satisfy you. For example, in some cases it is possible to determine what African ethnic group you're from through physical characteristics. This may be enough. But for others, an old story passed down through the family, such as the one Alex Haley traced, can provide a lead. Deed or plantation records can often provide a clue. If a slave was purchased directly from slave traders, his or her origin might be listed on the bill of sale or in the plantation's records.

The problems of tracing African-American genealogy are numerous. However, in my fifteen-year search I have overcome many obstacles and have met with great success. With proper guidance, many genealogists can successfully go back several generations. The purpose of this book is to provide a road map to your family's genealogical treasure; to help you find the information necessary to grow your very own family tree.

What do you already know about your family? Many of us may answer, "not much." When I began my genealogy search I could not name all four of my grandparents. Today I'm considered the family historian. Soon the same may be said about you. Genealogy is the fitting together of a person's ancestral puzzle. If you are reading this book, chances are you are the detective who will uncover clues to the missing pieces. "What do you already know about your family?" is an important question because a genealogist must work from the known to the unknown. The following are basic techniques for getting started.

Read a Book

This book is an excellent guide. There are, however, many other written resources that can aid your search. A recommended list is in the Appendix.

Join a Club

Contact genealogy clubs in your area. These clubs often provide beginners' lessons and can get you quickly moving in the right direction. As you become more experienced, genealogy clubs provide continued training and resources. Supportive clubs add camaraderie and fun to the research experience. My club sometimes travels to various research sites that provide valuable information. We often take our special guest speakers to dinner after the session. Any club member can join us on these outings. This gives members the opportunity to talk to these people and ask questions one on one. Clubs help add the human touch so that all the work is not field research. You get to meet and make friends with genealogists at all levels. Clubs also help to keep your motivation up. If no club exists near you, then join the national organization—the African-American Historical and Genealogical Society in Washington, D.C. There is a listing of various AAHGS chapters in the Appendix of this book.

START WITH YOURSELF

When people find out I'm a genealogist the first thing they usually say is, "I've been wanting to do that, how do I begin?" The answer is simple: work backward in time from yourself toward the unknown relatives. Write down information about yourself: where you were born; where you went to school; who you married; your hobbies, profession; and so on. Then do the same thing for your spouse, your parents, grandparents, great-grandparents, etc. To do a thorough job you'll need to trace both your father's and mother's family lines. As you work

My baby photograph from 1954. When beginning genealogy, start with yourself and work back in time to the unknown relatives. Author collection.

your way back through the generations, you'll have less and less information.

Begin with whatever information you have. This is your starting point on which the foundation of your research will be built. Next, you want to get a visual sense of your family tree; that necessitates genealogy charts.

Use Charts

Charts illustrate your family lineage. They provide you with quick access to individual ancestors' vital statistics, such as names and dates of birth, marriage, and death.

Charts can be purchased from genealogy supply houses listed in the resource guide in the back of this book. Reproducible charts are also available in handy genealogy resource books and through genealogy clubs. You can also make your own using the examples in this book. Charts that are $8^1/2 \times 11$ inches usually allow space for thirty-one names. Be sure to make several copies of the form.

There is a traditional numbering system used in genealogy. It may seem a little confusing at first, but when you've done it once it should be fairly clear. A sample chart is provided to show you an example of how it looks (Figure 1). Remember in genealogy you work from the known to the unknown, so start with yourself.

An ancestor's number never changes. Put yourself down as number 1. Your father is number 2, and your mother is number 3. As you continue to fill out the chart, your father's father is number 4, and your father's mother is number 5. Your mother's father is number 6, and your mother's mother is number 7. Your father's family goes on the lines above your name and your mother's family goes on the lines below your name.

If you need to continue your family ancestry beyond chart number 1, simply take another blank chart and label it chart number 2. This is a continuation of chart number 1. Don't be surprised if you're missing the names of ancestors from recent generations. This is the best place to begin, and gives you a clear look at what work needs to be done to complete the chart. You'll get a feeling of pride and accomplishment as you add more ancestors to your chart.

Fill in the dates and places you're sure about. It is best to write in pencil, since there are often name and date discrepancies from your various sources. Then information must be changed. Record vital information concerning your parents, grandparents, and other ancestors. Include full names, nicknames, birth dates, marriage dates, death dates, and places where the events took place. Write down all the data that you gather and cite the sources of each piece of information as you receive it. See the example in Figure 2.

CHART NUMBER_____

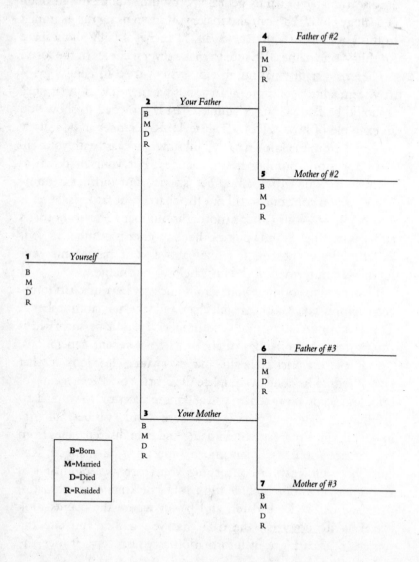

Figure 1: Ancestor Chart.

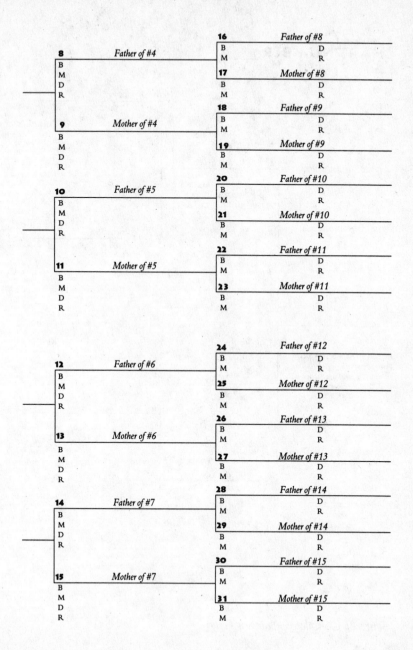

CHART NUMBER_____

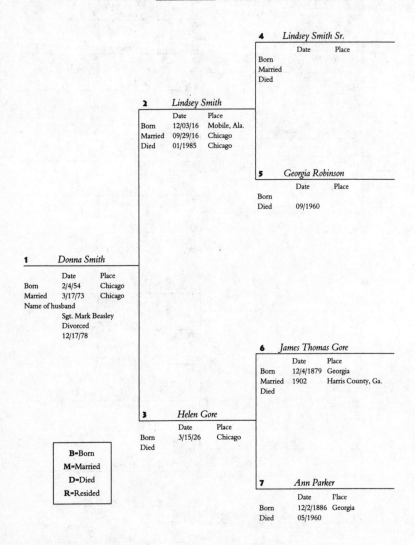

4   *Lindsey Smith Sr.*

	Date	Place
Born		
Married		
Died		

2   *Lindsey Smith*

	Date	Place
Born	12/03/16	Mobile, Ala.
Married	09/29/16	Chicago
Died	01/1985	Chicago

5   *Georgia Robinson*

	Date	Place
Born		
Died	09/1960	

1   *Donna Smith*

	Date	Place
Born	2/4/54	Chicago
Married	3/17/73	Chicago

Name of husband
Sgt. Mark Beasley
Divorced
12/17/78

6   *James Thomas Gore*

	Date	Place
Born	12/4/1879	Georgia
Married	1902	Harris County, Ga.
Died		

3   *Helen Gore*

	Date	Place
Born	3/15/26	Chicago
Died		

B=Born
M=Married
D=Died
R=Resided

7   *Ann Parker*

	Date	Place
Born	12/2/1886	Georgia
Died	05/1960	

Figure 2: Completed Ancestor Chart.

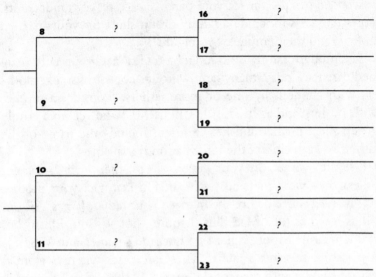

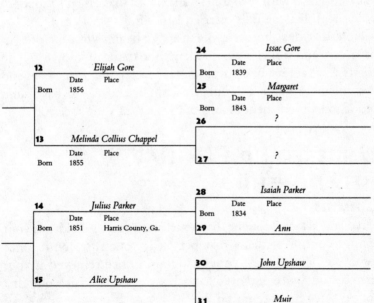

Fill out a group sheet for every married couple you are descended from—one for your parents, each set of grandparents, and so on. Also include a family group sheet for your married siblings and their families. See Figure 3.

The modern family is no longer a traditional group with married parents. Today, many family groups consist of single mothers with children by one or more fathers. Consider a mother with no husband as head of her household and record a family group sheet for her and her children. Include the name of the father for each child if the information is available.

List the women in your genealogy by their maiden names unless they were married twice. If, for example, your mother was married once before she married your father, James Wilson, she is listed as Julia Mae Ellis (Moore), not Wilson. Ellis is her maiden name; Moore is her first husband's name; and Wilson is her second husband's name. There are cases where a woman married a man with the same last name. In that case it's proper to note that Julia Mae Ellis married James Ellis.

Note that this approach to genealogy begins with the present or known and works its way back in time to the unknown. These charts serve at least two purposes: (1) to keep the family lines and descendants straight in your own mind; and (2) to have solid proof and a permanent record of the facts of your ancestors.

UNDERSTAND FAMILIAL RELATIONSHIPS
Cousins

Have you always thought that your first cousin's child was your second cousin? Actually that person is your first cousin once removed. The child of your first cousin once removed is your first cousin twice removed, and his or her child is your first cousin three times removed.

Your second cousin is your grandparent's brother or sister's grandchild. That second cousin's child is your second cousin

FAMILY GROUP CHART

Husband:
Born on:_____ At:_____
Died on:_____ At:_____
Buried on:_____ At:_____
Father:_____
Mother:_____

Wife:
Born on:_____ At:_____
Died on:_____ At:_____
Buried on:_____ At:_____
Father:_____
Mother:_____

Married on:_____ At:_____
Divorced on:_____
Number of children:_____

Child #1:   Gender:
Born on:_____ At:_____
Died on:_____ At:_____
Buried on:_____ At:_____
Married:_____ Date:_____

Child #2:   Gender:
Born on:_____ At:_____
Died on:_____ At:_____
Buried on:_____ At:_____
Married:_____ Date:_____

Figure 3.

once removed; his or her child is your second cousin twice removed, and so on.

Your third cousin is your great-grandparent's brother or sister's great-grandchild. The third cousin's child is your third cousin once removed and so on.

Great-Aunts and -Uncles

The sister or brother of a grandparent is your great-aunt or great-uncle. The sister or brother of a great-grandparent is your great-grand aunt or great-grand uncle. The grandchild of your brother or sister is your grandnephew or grandniece.

KEEP NOTES ORGANIZED

There are several ways of keeping the information organized; the most common are note cards, file folders, a loose-leaf notebook, or computer software. I personally like the file-folder method. You can number the folders or use names. In folder one goes your information: birth certificate, photograph, marriage license, and so on. Your father's documents go in folder two, and your mother's documents in folder three. Your father's parents documents go in folders four and five, your mother's parents documents go in folders six and seven. You don't need original documents— photocopies are fine. I name my folders for the person whose data it holds and include his or her number. Then I file the folders alphabetically. This way I can get to needed data quickly, especially since I can never remember if that ancestor's stuff is in folder five—or was it folder seven?

RECORD NAMES, DATES, PLACES, RELATIONSHIPS

You will be concerned with pulling these four key items from the many and varied documents of recorded history. These are the tools of the family researcher and the keys to your family's past. Always use letters, not numbers, for months. The reason for this is that your research may take you to other countries where the day is usually listed before the month. If you write 7/4/1856 meaning July 4, 1856, it would be misread as April seventh in some European cities or in parts of Africa or the Caribbean. If you write July 4, 1856, there can be no mistake.

USE HOME SOURCES

The place to begin is at home with your parents. From there, contact all living relatives and pump them for every scrap of genealogy information they possess. Tell them what you are doing and find out what information they can provide. Ask for copies of birth certificates, marriage licenses, and other important documents. The most valuable leads will come from interviewing relatives and reviewing newspaper clippings, military papers, marriage licenses, diaries, and scrapbooks. A wealth of information comes from these documents.

Relatives

You should write a letter, pay a personal visit, or conduct a telephone survey to those in your family who may have information, particularly older relatives.

While each of us must decide on our own approach, some decisions have tough consequences. I chose to do my mother's family first. There was so much research involved, and it took me years. I never interviewed my father even though I was in the same house with him most of the time. My father died before I got to his side of the family tree. As a result, I lost a valuable resource. There are gaps in his family's history I may never be able to fill.

In African villages a griot is the person responsible for keeping the oral history of a village and its inhabitants. In Africa, they say when a griot dies it is like losing a library. I feel that same way about an elderly relative. Interview your parents, grandparents, and oldest relatives first.

It is often difficult to get African-American families to write or respond through the mail. I find that telephone and personal visits work best. When interviewing an elderly or reluctant relative, plan a face-to-face visit when possible. The interviewees need to feel they can trust you with this information and that you're not just a strange voice on the phone. It means more to them when Aunt Hazel's grandson comes to visit them in person. They're usually glad to see you and more forthcoming with the needed information.

Don't overlook collateral relatives and friends. In genealogy, anyone who is not in your direct line of ancestry is considered a collateral. Your father's brother is a collateral relative because he is not on your ancestor chart. In my personal search, however, I considered a collateral any individual who was not related to me but who knew a lot about my family. For example, my maternal grandfather was a minister. I learned a lot about his ministry and some of my relatives from his church secretary, who eventually married into the family.

Collect Important Family Documents

Collect old photographs and documents that you discover in your search. Relatives may not want to part with them. Let them know you'll duplicate the photos and return them quickly. Give them a receipt to help instill confidence. Documents you may discover include family Bibles and diaries. I found a wonderful family document lying dormant for years in my own basement. Let me explain.

Growing up, whenever my family members would mention my mother's brother, Uncle Ben, they would always discuss

My grandparents, Reverend James Gore with his wife, Ann (Parker) Gore, in 1947, on the fortieth anniversary of Friendship Baptist Church, which my grandfather founded and pastored. Surrounding the couple are twenty-six of their grandchildren. The couple's twenty children eventually blessed them with sixty-six grandchildren, most of whom had not been born when this photograph was taken. Author Collection.

World War II. The story goes my uncle Ben was an outstanding soldier who became the youngest sergeant ever at Fort Custer. His job was to train his men to use the big guns. What big guns? Something called "millimeters" said one aunt, but nobody really knew. In 1985, after my father's death, I was cleaning out his old military trunk, which he still had from the war. It contained his yearbook from training camp. I didn't know they had yearbooks back then. I knew my father and Ben were good friends and served in the Illinois militia together. When the war broke out they were both activated into the Army. As I went through the book I discovered my father and Uncle Ben had trained together but in different units.

They served in an all-Negro unit, the 184th Field Artillery, the First Battalion, stationed at Fort Custer, Michigan. My father was a field communications expert, and as oral history said Uncle Ben was a gunner. He was an expert on the 75mm gun and the 155mm howitzer. The 75mm weighed three thousand pounds and was capable of projecting a fifteen-pound weight over nine thousand yards. The gun, a most effective antitank weapon, prepared the way for quick offensive infantry moves. The massive 155mm howitzer, weighing twenty-eight thousand pounds, fired a ninety-pound projectile seventeen thousand yards (almost ten miles). It took a crew of ten men to efficiently operate the gun and fire it four times per minute. The book even had pictures of the guns.

Using my father's military discharge papers, the yearbook, and some notes he had written in the back of the book, I was able to assemble a good picture of my father's military career. Thus, family documents can be invaluable sources of research data.

Use Public Information Sources
Federal Records

The National Archives and Records Administration is the federal government agency responsible for preserving federal records and making them available for research. This agency's records document American history from the first Continental Congress. The population census from 1790 to 1920 is the most valuable for tracing family history. They are available on microfilm. Besides the main building in Washington, D.C., there are many branch offices where you can view the microfilm files. A listing of these sites is in the Appendix of this book.

Census Records

The first U.S. census was taken in 1790. Only the heads of families are named. Each subsequent census obtained more information. The 1800 and 1810 census include head of family, number of free white males and females and all other free persons, except Indians and slaves. The 1820 census lists persons, including slaves, engaged in agriculture, commerce, and manufacturing. The 1840 census added Revolutionary War pensioners and ages. The 1850 census was the first census that named everyone living in the family and their place of birth. The 1850 and 1860 censuses are basically alike and both include slave schedules (a listing of slaves by sex and age only). More information about using these censuses is given in chapter three under the section "Using the Census." Additionally, the 1850, 1860, and 1870 censuses include information on who died within the twelve months prior to the census taking. These lists are known as the Mortality Schedules. Almost all, 99 percent, of the 1890 census was destroyed by fire. Try using veterans records to fill in information gaps.

Amazingly, some people never get counted in the census system. I have a friend, a Vietnam veteran, who does not have a birth certificate and can't obtain one because he can't find three official documents (the requirement) that give the same date of his birth. Even his three children's birth certificates all have a different birth date listed for their father. Also, his immediate family never participated in the census when he was growing up. The climb up his family tree will include overcoming these obstacles.

But my friend's family is not rare. The undercount of African-American households in the census has been a bone of contention for legislators and census takers since 1870. If you cannot find a direct ancestor in the census information, try tracing a brother or sister of that ancestor.

Social Security Records

The Social Security Administration began keeping records in 1936. You may be able to obtain a copy of your deceased ancestor's original application for a Social Security card. This application is usually in the applicant's own handwriting, and gives his or her name, date of birth, place of birth, and parents' names. As noted, the individual must be deceased in order for you to request this information. There is a fee charged for this search. Write to the Social Security Administration, 4-C-5 Annex Building, 6401 Security Boulevard, Baltimore, MD 21235.

Birth, Marriage, and Death Records

Some states and counties began to keep records of births and deaths before the turn of the century, but for most of the United States birth and death documentation were not required until after 1900. Before then, such events were generally documented only in church records and in personal family records.

Many African-American children born prior to 1920 were delivered by midwives instead of doctors. Often, the only record of the birth was in the family Bible, which may no longer exist. If your ancestor has no birth certificate, you may have to use other sources, such as census, school, and Social Security records to estimate his or her age.

Sometimes records are destroyed. All the birth and death records from the 1800s were burned in a fire in the Georgia county I was researching. Marriage records will be found in most counties, often dating back to the establishment of the county. Remember that in most counties the record of marriages among Negroes was listed in a separate book from white marriages. Only free black marriages were recorded before the end of slavery. Slaves could not marry legally, although many improvised and had wedding ceremonies like "Jumping the Broom." This symbolic action united them before God and their slave family.

Church Records

Church records, when available, can be a great resource in tracing African-American genealogy. Most people attended a church close to home, although not every community had a church building. Many ministers in the South traveled from community to community in the years after slavery. Few records probably exist. However, if your ancestors are like some of mine—that is, they were ministers—then church records may be available.

Deeds and Wills

Records of property acquisition and disposition can be good sources of genealogical data. Such records are normally in county courthouses. Often the earliest county records or copies of them are also available in state archives. During my research of the courthouse records in Harris County, Georgia, where my family came from, I struck gold. While it was easy for me to find the Parker plantation, it was a lot harder to prove that my ancestor had been a slave on that plantation. Finding the link to my white ancestor helped me in my courthouse search. Let me explain.

Isaiah Parker Sr. was the plantation owner. Parker's son, Isaiah Jr., established a common-law marriage with a slave girl named Ann. Together they had several children during slavery. However, Ann and the children remained the property of the elder Parker. When the elder Parker suddenly died without a will, his estate went into probate court. The court authorized a detailed appraisal of his property. This included every slave by name and his or her value. I was able to locate Ann and her children in the appraisal records of the probate court. Often, however, there are no official records of these children. At the most, the word *infant* or *child* appears after the mother's name.

The courthouse records are a wonderful place to search for legal documents. During my visit to the Harris County courthouse, besides the probate records, I also found a copy of my grandparents' marriage license, my great-grandparents' homestead exemption application, which listed all of their personal property in detail, and a deed in which my great-great-grandfather (the aforementioned Isaiah Parker Jr.) gave a gift of a horse and her colt to his loving wife Ann several years after the Civil War.

Libraries

Genealogical resources are available in major libraries. These collections include manuscripts, family papers, Civil War research collections, and local history. Additionally, there are several libraries that specialize in genealogy. In the Midwest, the Newberry Library in Chicago, Illinois, and the Allen County Library in Fort Wayne, Indiana, are excellent resources. For example, the Allen County Library's renowned collection contains more than 181,000 volumes and 220,000 items on microfiche. It also holds 38,000 volumes of compiled genealogies and family histories. These special libraries also have city directories, military records including those from the Revolutionary War, War of 1812, and the Civil War, as well as local records.

Most genealogy libraries have specific research sources for tracing African-American family history. When I started my genealogy search, the Newberry Library had little information of benefit to African-American researchers. That has changed, Today, the Newberry Library and many others have hundreds of sources for African-American researchers. For example, the Newberry's collection includes the following:

- Federal census slaves schedules for 1850 and 1860
- Records of antebellum Southern plantations from the revolution through the Civil War
- Freedman Bureau records
- Pennsylvania Abolition Society papers
- Slave manumission county courthouse records for some states
- State slavery statutes

The Library of Congress is the national public library located in Washington, D.C. It has a large collection of historical and genealogical information on African-Americans. One of the library's historical documents is the book *The African-American Mosaic*. It is for sale in the bookstore.

There are many other research libraries that have valuable information. These include the New England Historic Genealogical Society in Boston; the Confederate Research Center in Hillsboro, Texas; and the Family History Library of the Church of Jesus Christ of Latter-Day Saints in Salt Lake City, Utah.

The Family History Library in Salt Lake City has an incredible amount of information, probably the largest private collection. Best of all you don't have to go there to access the information. Just visit a Family History Center (FHC), which is a branch of the library. These centers can be found all over the world. They are located near or inside buildings of the Church of Jesus Christ of Latter-Day Saints. FHCs are open to the public and are run like a library. Anything not held in the collection of the center near you can be ordered from the main library in Salt Lake City. There is usually a small shipping and handling fee and the records will be held for two weeks. To find one near you look in the phone book for a church and call to get a nearby location.

Don't overlook local county libraries as a source of research. I had heard about a book called *The History of Harris County, Georgia 1827–1961* by Louise Calhoun Barfield. I had been unable to obtain a copy until my visit to the Harris County library. Not only was the book on the shelf to borrow, but additional copies were for sale at the library. I was able to secure a personal copy. Although African-Americans are barely mentioned in the book, it has been an excellent resource on land, typography, maps, early churches, a clear reproduction of the county's 1850 census, land records of some white slaveholders, plus historical information on the county.

As you trace your family back in time you'll need to get a sense of history, some understanding of the time and place your ancestors lived. Libraries have a wealth of historical information on the period of slavery, Reconstruction, and the great migration of blacks to Northern cities. Some public libraries in the African-American community specialize in black research and/or genealogy. Call the genealogy department of the main library in your city for the names and locations of these special branch libraries.

Once you trace through the census and find ancestors on your family tree you'll be curious about who these people were and how they lived. The best way to obtain this information is from relatives who knew them or heard about them. The next chapter provides some key interviewing guidelines. So come on, there is so much more to discover as you continue to embark on this exciting treasure hunt.

ORAL HISTORY

HISTORY OF THE GRIOT

Passing the story of one's family on to the next generation is an African tradition that is still practiced today. African griots memorize the genealogy and history of their tribes. The honor of being the village griot is passed from one generation to the next. The position must be inherited.

Since most slaves could neither read nor write, the history of plantation life, and stories of slaves bought and sold, were passed orally. By conducting oral interviews you'll be keeping this tradition alive in your own family. You'll become the family griot. This is my favorite part of tracing my family's history. Relatives are a gold mine of information, funny stories, gossip, and tall tales.

Oral history is intriguing. Two people can tell the same story and remember it differently. Age, frame of mind, and how personally one was affected all play a role in how a person remembers his or her past. So if two of your relatives don't remember a story quite the same way, it's all right. It is each individual's interpretation you want to capture. Of course, it is impossible to document a person's life in a one- or two-hour interview. But it's a wonderful snapshot into his or her life and times.

Developing a Family Heritage

The purpose of collecting oral history is to move beyond the facts of your genealogy to develop a family heritage. I have seen many family genealogies that are names, dates, and locations only. While they may be accurate portrayals of a family's lineage, they are boring to read. Producing a family heritage is a much more exciting pursuit. And when you publish your findings, they are more exciting to read.

For example, I can tell you that my grandparents had twenty children and list them by name. That, however, won't give you the same insight you'd gain from someone who grew up in a household with nineteen siblings.

My aunt Margaret describes it this way: "When I was growing up it was chaotic with all those brothers and sisters. We'd be five or six in the bed, kicking each other, fighting about who peed on you at night. We slept in our clothes and nubie caps [skullcaps] because it was so cold. There was me, Sam, Julius, Jack, Anna Mae; they didn't separate the boys from the girls."

According to Aunt Dolly: "It was a bunch of us, but we were not all in the house at the same time when I was coming along at about age eight. Some of them were grown, married, and gone like Melinda, Minnie, and Anna Mae. Some of them weren't born yet like Helen, Rita, and Richard. Our apartments were like large seven- or eight-room flats, and we had three or four fireplaces. You cooked with coal and wood so the kitchen and dining room was always warm. We had one big, black potbelly stove in the front, so we kept pretty warm.

"We took baths in these big tubs, as big as a table. We'd get the dishes cleaned up from dinner and get ready for our baths. My mother would heat the water twice a week in large metal tubs. We'd burn coal and wood in the stove until the water got hot. We took baths two at a time because you had to heat all that water. On the days between baths we washed up. My mother made us wash our feet every night. I never remember my mother letting us go to bed with dirty feet. Those days the water would be cold, you didn't get hot water for a wash-up."

My aunt Mary remembered: "Growing up as preacher's daughters we couldn't do what we had in mind to do. We had to obey the elders. My daddy wouldn't let us wear bobby socks and silk stockings, which were popular back then. We wore them real cotton stockings and long underwear. Sometimes we'd be so ashamed going to school. Me and Margaret would go down the steps and when Mama couldn't see us anymore we'd take off those long draws."

Here is my mother Helen remembering her mother: "I remember having fun with Mama playing softball and games. She could really play ball. Bingo was a favorite game and so was Peanuts. We had to guess how many peanuts was in the pile. If you could guess them, you could have them. We would be trying to get those peanuts. We had fun playing with Mama."

Now don't these recollections give you a better understanding of what the sisters' lives were like? Sure it's only a snapshot, but it gives you a sense of their day-to-day lives, their feelings and their joys. That is what you want to seek as you develop your family's heritage—the story of families, yours and mine.

BUILDING A FOUNDATION

Genealogy is the foundation on which you build. You must know who these people are or were, where they lived and when. From this, you can develop a questionnaire and interview schedule.

Begin with yourself. After all, you are a member of this family and as much a keeper of family traditions as any other member. You'd be surprised at what you know already about your family. You may even practice traditions that were passed down from your parents and that you are now passing on to your children.

Write down what you know about your family. Include any favorite family traditions, fond memories of your parents, grandparents, brothers, sisters, aunts, uncles, cousins, and any other relatives you deem important in your life. Develop questions for the unknown information for which you'd like to find answers. It doesn't have to be only important memories and events. Include some light fun moments as well.

For example, my fraternal grandmother Georgia made fantastic melt-in-your-mouth pancakes. She has been dead for more than thirty years. However, she taught my brother Charles how to make those pancakes. And whenever I'm invited, I hightail it to his house for breakfast. The aroma of frying bacon whiffing through the house; the sizzle of Grandma's pancake batter recipe hitting the grill; the smell of ground-roasted coffee pouring into my cup, and butter-strewn pancakes, generously lathered with Alaga syrup, melting in my mouth. These are part of a favorite, good-tasting tradition still practiced in my family. I grew up on Alaga syrup, which is much thicker than maple syrup and still preferred by me and many African-American households.

As you move on to interview other family members, remember you definitely want the genealogical facts: when they were born, where they grew up, where they went to school and worked, and so on. You also want to capture what they remember about their parents and grandparents. Don't overlook cousins, uncles, and aunts. My grandparents were dead long before I began my search. Luckily, both my maternal grandmother and maternal grandfather had living sisters who were most helpful. Interview all such elderly relatives as early as possible in your research.

In addition to the facts, you also want to know about their life experiences. The key is to capture both the details of the family history and the spirit of the family heritage. What were their accomplishments or disappointments? What brought them joy or pain? How do they feel about their country, past presidents, mayors, and other civic leaders? Were they active in the civil rights movement? What was their experience with racism? Did they serve in any wars, and if so, how did it affect their lives? How did they survive the Great Depression? What role did religion play in their life? What did they do for fun and entertainment? These are just a few examples of the kinds of questions that get to the heart of life experiences.

USING FAMILY REUNIONS

Family reunions are one of the best sources for interviewing relatives. Although a tradition among black families since slavery, the growing interest in one's ancestors and family has caused an explosion of family reunions among African-Americans. Literally thousands of family reunions are held each summer. In 1993 *Black Enterprise* magazine reported 45 percent of African-Americans travel to a family reunion each year.

It is very difficult to get African-American family members to fill out information questionnaires sent through the mail. At family reunions you can speak directly with each relative while you fill out the form or otherwise record their responses. At one family reunion I set up a video camera and recorded the senior members of the family. They are the last of their generation, and I wanted their faces and voices on camera for my genealogy research collection.

Often African-Americans relatives, particularly the elderly, don't feel their lives were of value or that they made any contributions worth discussing. And they certainly don't think of their lives in any historical context.

The key with reluctant relatives is to assure them you are not seeking great events from their past. You only want to know what life was like when they were growing up. Let them know there are no right and wrong answers. You just want to take a stroll with them down memory lane. Begin with their childhood memories and go from there. People usually warm up and get into the spirit of the interview as they begin talking about their life as a child, and their fond memories of parents and siblings.

Also, remember that at family reunions, one relative can help spark another in revealing aspects of their lives or the telling of tall tales or humorous anecdotes. Don't head for a family reunion without taking your camera, your notepad, and your tape recorder. Your job as the family historian is to learn your family's heritage and record it for others to enjoy.

The following suggestions are designed to help you get started on interviewing for your family's history and heritage.

EQUIPMENT NEEDS
Tape Recorder

Note taking and tape recording are the usual means of documenting oral interviews. I use them both. The tape recorder is best because it is hard to participate in a lively discussion and take notes at the same time. It is also easier to maintain visual contact with the person being interviewed. Sometimes a relative's story is long and filled with details. Thus, a complete and accurate account would be difficult and painstaking to record by hand.

A small, voice-activated cassette recorder is excellent and inconspicuous. Soon you won't notice that it is in the room. I find the ones that use the mini-cassettes difficult to transcribe from. I personally prefer a tape recorder that uses the traditional full-size cassette tapes. This gives more flexibility in using a variety of machines for playback. Sometimes I've had to get a better quality cassette player for greater clarity of voices, particularly those of the elderly. With mini-cassettes you're usually locked into the one machine with which you recorded. However, I've used both types of machines quite successfully. Also, using headphones when transcribing can be helpful if you need greater sound clarity for that process.

Be sure you test the machine before your interview begins. The end of your session is a sorry time to find out you forgot to hit record, turn up the volume, or put a tape in the machine. Also try to eliminate background noises. I interviewed my uncle Jack and left his TV going in the background. We didn't even notice it during the interview since it was in another room. But when it came time to transcribe that tape it was painstaking and time-consuming to pick up his words over the sounds of the television.

Notepad

Don't rely on the tape recorder only; take your notepad. The pad comes in handy if you run out of tape before you run out of interview. I've had interviews that were supposed to be two hours that ran four. Woe the person without pen and paper at a time like that. I always write down the facts of birth dates, deaths, marriages, names and ages of children, and so on. That way I have that information at my fingertips and don't have to transcribe a tape to get it.

Some of my interviews, unintentionally, involved two or three people at a time. For example, during my interview with Aunt Margaret, her daughter Bonnie and son-in-law Bill stopped by for a visit. This is not a problem as long as one person talks at a time. As a matter of fact, Bill added some interesting background and insight on what was happening during the 1920s and 1930s, particularly from a black man's perspective. This was a viewpoint that my aunt could not have provided.

DETERMINING WHOM TO INTERVIEW

Determine which relatives or collateral people are likely to have the information you need. Remember, interviewing older members of the family is a priority. In-person interviews are the best to obtain local information. Long-distance telephone calls are expensive but can save time and are great when you can't travel to an out-of-town location. Letters are economical but may yield little or no information because some relatives may be reluctant to write. Any written inquiries should be short and to the point.

Conducting the Interviews

Make an appointment and go to your interview prepared and on time. Have a list of questions already written down. Be sure to ask open-ended questions that require more than just a "yes" or "no" answer. Open-ended questions provide a fun and provocative discussion. Too many yes-or-no questions can kill an interview. Bring your family's history chart for reference during the interview.

I have a wonderful collection of old family photographs that I show before my interview. It's a good conversation starter and always sends my relatives strolling down memory lane. Other props may be just as effective. Use old letters, scrapbooks, family Bibles, and the like.

Be a good listener. You want to actively participate in the discussion without dominating it. Show interest in the person's comments and encourage him or her to talk as much as possible.

Using a Questionnaire

The following guidelines will help you develop a questionnaire. These are, however, just suggestions. The most useful questions will be those you develop through your knowledge of your family.

Get the Facts

Record the basic family historical information. This includes names, dates, places of birth, marriages, and so on. Include any nicknames.

Record descriptions of ancestors, including their physical characteristics, personality traits, distinguishing features, and the like.

Ask interviewees if they saved obituaries. Review and collect these if they are available.

Ask if there are any old photos that you can have, borrow, and/or duplicate.

Ask if there are any old family Bibles, scrapbooks, or similar documents that you can review.

Ask interviewees where they worked and went to school. Ask about their social habits.

Get the Heritage

Gather information about the time period in which they lived, such as the Roaring Twenties, the Harlem Renaissance, or the Big Band era.

One interesting story in my family tells how enterprising my aunt and uncle were during Prohibition. The sale of alcohol was prohibited in the United States, but many people purchased alcohol on the black market. My Aunt Margaret and Uncle Hilton took advantage of this by setting up their own whiskey still in their living room. It was quite a lucrative business. My aunt explained the details of the family business this way:

It was 1933 or so, and we made good money selling whiskey. We ran three barrels of moonshine. We made 100-proof whiskey. But we bought gin essence and diluted our 100-proof down to a gin-proof level and cooked that with the gin essence. Shine was clear but we always put in barrels; that gave it color. But you could get it clear if you wanted it. We put the whiskey in containers like hot water bottles. People would place orders. A quart was fifty cents, a half-gallon was a dollar, and a gallon two dollars. To deliver the moonshine, I loaded it in my baby's carriage up under the baby, making deliveries door-to-door and walking the baby at the same time. When Prohibition ended it didn't put us out of business. People wanted moonshine; they had gotten used to it.

Ask about the stories that have been passed on to the interviewees about their parents and grandparents. How did the various couples meet?

Are there any notorious or infamous family members? Are there any stories of unusual marriages, lost loves, elopements, broken hearts, and/or betrayals? What about long-lasting marriages and great love affairs?

Were there any unusual funerals? Don't laugh. My family tells me when my maternal grandmother died, there were so many cars in the funeral procession, the Chicago city police had to block off the streets from the funeral home to the cemetery until the funeral procession went by. The cars numbered well over a hundred. This was our final tribute to a woman who had twenty children, sixty-six grandchildren, hundreds of great-grandchildren, and a host of other relatives and friends.

You never know what you might find out about your family's funerals, so ask. Is there a family cemetery or burial plot? Who is buried there?

Who are the great cooks in the family? Are there any good family recipes to share?

Are there any great poets, writers, storytellers, singers, dancers, or other entertainers in the family?

Are there any friends that are like family? These are important collateral friends and should be interviewed.

Do any family members belong to clubs and fraternities, such as the Alpha Kappa Alpha, Kappa Psi Phi, and Sigma Gamma Rho? Are they members of the Masons, Eastern Stars, or other benevolent organizations? You are not trying to pry into any sacred rites of these organizations. Rather you are trying to find out if any organizations played an active role in an ancestor's life. The clubs, fraternities, and sororities family members join tell you a little about them: such as that they probably enjoyed people, tended to be social, and took pride in being able to join a prestigious group of like-minded people. If they were officers in these organizations that tells you they may have had leadership qualities. By joining organizations, your ancestors are telling you that they are part of a national brotherhood or sisterhood.

When I interviewed my cousin, who is a Mason, he shared the following reflection about his father, also a Mason.

My father's been a Mason as long as I can remember. I have records in my basement that showed Daddy was a Mason as far back as 1947. We were trained not to touch his Masonic books. We never got too curious to look in them Masonic books because we knew Daddy would get us good. The only person who could touch them was Mama, and she could only move them to clean. He was a thirty-third-degree Mason, the highest you can attain. Daddy belonged to the National Supreme Council of Ancient Accepted Scottish Rite Masons of the World. He helped build the National Supreme Council. He was one of the smartest Masons on the globe to me. He knew its rituals, he knew it biblically, and he knew both the male side and the female side. The female side is the Eastern Stars. My mother was an Eastern Star.

Obviously, the Masons played a major role in my uncle's life. Can you feel the serious commitment my uncle had to this organization? Can you sense the pride he felt as a member? I can even feel the pride my cousin has for both his father's accomplishment within the organization and for being a Mason himself—a bond they shared. A greater understanding of an individual is what you're seeking to capture as you explore an ancestor's group affiliations.

Are there any relatives or ancestors involved in politics? Any relatives with a criminal past? Ask who did it and why.

What were holidays such as Christmas, Easter, and Halloween like when the interviewee was a child? What happened to make these events memorable?

Ask about the interviewee's grammar school and high school career. What clothes were worn when he or she was growing up?

Finally, ask if the interviewees know of anyone else in the family who is doing or has done a family history. If so, find that person and exchange information.

Genealogist Elizabeth Shown Mills said, "A human life is a continuous, cohesive, compatible chain; and the links which form that chain are people, events, and patterns of behavior." Oral history is the tool that will help you go beyond the people to capture the events and patterns of behavior in your family's heritage.

Much of your spare time over the next few years will be spent navigating the courthouse, libraries, and archives of this country digging up your family treasures. At each port of call you'll experience new discoveries and surprises. As an African-American genealogist, the further you go back in history the more obstacles you'll need to overcome. The next chapter will focus on these obstacles and the research sources that can help you hurdle over them.

SLAVERY—THE TIE
THAT BINDS US

"There is one subject that deepens my sorrow, perpetuates my pain, escapes my understanding and confuses my perception. It is a phenomenon in the life of our people that showed no mercy, provided no justice, and prevailed no good in its entire existence. . . . My soul cries out for a small measure of insight into its meaning." These are the words of genealogist Carlotta Campbell as she described the history of slavery in "Our Family," her family's newsletter.

HOW SLAVERY DEVELOPED

The first slaves came to North America in 1619 and were indentured servants under work contracts. It would be several decades before slaves began to arrive in large numbers. The demand for slaves, especially in the South, was fueled by the need to cultivate crops such as tobacco, rice, and sugarcane.

Most slaves were brought from Africa's west coast. Historians have estimated that one out of every six or eight slaves forced aboard a ship in Africa never landed in America. It is also reported that sharks often followed slave ships, feeding on bodies tossed overboard. Slavery was a very profitable business and grew quickly. By 1860 the slave states had almost four million slaves. There were also about 480,000 free Negroes.

BY

HEWLETT & BRIGHT.

SALE OF

VALUABLE

SLAVES,

(On account of departure)

The Owner of the following named and valuable Slaves, being on the eve of departure for Europe, will cause the same to be offered for sale, at the NEW EXCHANGE, corner of St. Louis and Chartres streets, on *Saturday*, May 16, at Twelve o'Clock, *viz.*

1. SARAH, a mulatress, aged 45 years, a good cook and accustomed to house work in general, is an excellent and faithful nurse for sick persons, and in every respect a first rate character.

2. DENNIS, her son, a mulatto, aged 24 years, a first rate cook and steward for a vessel, having been in that capacity for many years on board one of the Mobile packets; is strictly honest, temperate, and a first rate subject.

3. CHOLE, a mulatress, aged 36 years, she is, without exception, one of the most competent servants in the country, a first rate washer and ironer, does up lace, a good cook, and for a bachelor who wishes a house-keeper she would be invaluable; she is also a good ladies' maid, having travelled to the North in that capacity.

4. FANNY, her daughter, a mulatress, aged 16 years, speaks French and English, is a superior hair-dresser, (pupil of Guilliac,) a good seamstress and ladies' maid, is smart, intelligent, and a first rate character.

5. DANDRIDGE, a mulatoo, aged 26 years, a first rate dining-room servant, a good painter and rough carpenter, and has but few equals for honesty and sobriety.

6. NANCY, his wife, aged about 24 years, a confidential house servant, good seamstress, mantuamaker and tailoress, a good cook, washer and ironer, etc.

7. MARY ANN, her child, a creole, aged 7 years, speaks French and English, is smart, active and intelligent.

8. FANNY or FRANCES, a mulatress, aged 22 years, is a first rate washer and ironer, good cook and house servant, and has an excellent character.

9. EMMA, an orphan, aged 10 or 11 years, speaks French and English, has been in the country 7 years, has been accustomed to waiting on table, sewing etc.; is intelligent and active.

10. FRANK, a mulatto, aged about 32 years speaks French and English, is a first rate hostler and coachman, understands perfectly well the management of horses, and is, in every respect, a first rate character, with the exception that he will occasionally drink, though not an habitual drunkard.

☞ All the above named Slaves are acclimated and excellent subjects; they were purchased by their present vendor many years ago, and will, therefore, be severally warranted against all vices and maladies prescribed by law, save and except FRANK, who is fully guaranteed in every other respect but the one above mentioned.

TERMS:—One-half Cash, and the other half in notes at Six months, drawn and endorsed to the satisfaction of the Vendor, with special mortgage on the Slaves until final payment. The Acts of Sale to be passed before WILLIAM BOSWELL, *Notary Public*, at the expense of the Purchaser.

New-Orleans, May 13, 1835.

PRINTED BY BENJAMIN LEVY.

This poster is typical of the kind used to announce a public auction of slaves. Collection of The New York Historical Society.

Your Slave Ancestors

Your ancestors endured the long trip to America, known as the Middle Passage. Upon arrival, they were put on the auction block and sold like property.

There was no effort on the part of slave buyers or sellers to keep African families intact. Husbands and wives were separated, and children were often sold to different plantations than their parents. Only very young children were allowed to stay with their mothers. Slaves had no knowledge of which county, plantation, or state their family members were heading for. This separation was usually final, and these family members never saw each other again.

You must remember that only the best and strongest Africans were selected; and only the strongest of these survived the trauma of the slave ship; and only the best of the best could survive the horror of slavery. That tells me that your African ancestor is the root of a very strong and powerful family tree—yours.

Slavery is our common link in the chain of our African-American history. It was, however, just a historical fact until I met my slave ancestors among historical documents. Slavery has a greater personal impact when that slave is your great-great-grandmother or -grandfather. It can bring tears to your eyes when you get a sense of his or her pain and hardship. It can also make you very proud to be a descendant.

They hung in there, persevered, prayed, had faith there would be a better day, dreamed of a better life for their children, raised beautiful children both black and white, seized opportunity when they could, schemed to endure it, escaped from it, worked to end it, and survived to pass on a legacy about which we genealogists can write. As a researcher tracing your slave ancestors, you will have unique problems to overcome.

How to Find Your Slave Ancestors' Plantation

In tracing your genealogy it is important to find the household or plantation where your ancestors were enslaved. Armed with this essential bit of information, you can learn much about their lives.

Using Old Censuses

Begin with the census in the state your family is from and research back through the 1870 census. From that report pull any location information such as county, township, district, and so on. You can find the censuses on microfilm at regional branch offices of the National Archives and many libraries. Most African-American families lived in the same areas after slavery as they did during slavery (that is, prior to 1865). This method gives you a defined area to begin your search.

Your goal is twofold: first, to find the slaveholder's family name and location of his farm or plantation; and second, to find written documentation that your family members worked or were slaves on that plantation.

Check to see if there are any white families with the same last name as yours. Next examine those names that are spelled differently but sound alike: for example, Gore or Gorr. Remember that the enumerators who took the census were not always accurate and often spelled a family name the way it sounded. Once you have established the slaveholder's name, begin to focus on both public and private written records and documents. Track the slaveholder back through the 1850 and 1860 census to get as much information as you can.

Look for the slaveholder's name on the 1850 and 1860 slave census. This will verify whether or not he owned slaves. If he did, you may be able to find out how many slaves and sometimes how many slave houses were on the plantation. Knowing

Slave cabins like the one depicted above were just one room, usually with dirt floors, that held cots or a makeshift pad on which slaves slept. Several people lived in each cabin. Collection of The New York Historical Society.

the number of slaves and slave houses gives you a good indication of the size of the farm or plantation. For example, if the slave owner had only one slave, he probably had a small business or a farm he operated himself. On the other hand, if he has two hundred slaves and twenty-five slave houses, then you know this was a large operating plantation. If any slaves had a special skill such as blacksmithing or carpentry, it may be listed on the slave census.

In the slave census for the Parker family, I discovered they owned twenty-one slaves, ages one to thirty-five, who lived in six slave houses. The 1860 census reported the real estate to be valued at six thousand dollars, and the total Parker estate to be worth eighteen thousand. This was considered a rich family in those days.

Your next research stop will be public records for the slave-holder.

INFORMATION SOURCES

The sources mentioned in the previous section outline basic information on how to begin to find the slave plantation. The following information goes a step further and includes several public record resources that can be of great value in tracing African-American family history during slavery.

Estate Records

Estate and probate court records are among the most valuable for identifying slaves on plantations. These records are available at state archives. If the slaveholder left a will, he may have mentioned your ancestors by name, especially if he left them to a relative. In some cases, the will granted slaves their freedom.

If the slaveholder died intestate, that is, without leaving a will, his estate probably had to go through probate courts, which would often order an appraisal of all property. In this document every item was listed and valued. Slaves were often listed by name and value. Sometimes physical descriptions, ages, and sex were also included in the assessment. When the appraiser filed his report with the court it was called a *return*. When reviewing court records, be sure to check all returns.

Don't expect this information to always be available neatly organized and categorized and awaiting your arrival at the county courthouse. You may have to dig some of this information out of its hiding places. I found the court records for my ancestor's estate in dusty boxes in a back room of a county courthouse. I had to patiently go through several books before I found the gold mine of information that was hidden within. When you visit a local courthouse don't be afraid of a little dust or getting yourself dirty kneeling on the floor.

Land Records

Most slaveholders owned property, and land records include deeds and mortgages. Generally, these provide the date of the deed, the grantee's (purchaser's) full name, his county or place of residence, and a description of the land and its location. The person selling the land is called a *grantor*. You can look up these records by either the grantor or grantee's name.

Usually land records are housed with the recorder of deeds at the local county courthouse. Often, however, you can find this same information on microfilm at the appropriate state archive. You can also write and request a search of these records. Most archives will accommodate your request for a small fee.

It was easy to trace my grandfather's family back to 1870 in Harris County, Georgia, but there the line ran out. I knew from oral history that my ancestors were in that county during the period of slavery and prior to 1860. It was common practice for slaves to take the name of their owners and my family name, Gore, is unique in that county. Following the end of slavery, the Gores were sharecroppers. Historical research on the reconstruction of Georgia convinced me that my ancestors were sharecroppers on the same land where they had been slaves—in the lower nineteenth district of Harris County. Yet for many years I could never find proof of a slave owner named Gore in Harris County.

An oral history story that I had ignored years back resurfaced in a recent interview. The story claimed our family name had been Smith but the plantation was bought out by a man named Gore. On my next trip to Atlanta I followed up on this lone lead at the Georgia State Archives, and there among the deed records was the bill of sale. I discovered, however, that Pharis Gore's property was seized by the sheriff and sold at auction. The buyer was Sidney Smith, who was the highest bidder at one hundred dollars. The property was located in the lower nineteenth district of Harris County. Bingo! I was on to something. This lead is one I'm still following up on as I write this book.

Bills of Sale

When non-real estate property was exchanged, a bill of sale was usually created. This would be true for purchasing slaves. A record of the slave sale may provide additional information on your ancestors. This sale was also recorded in deed books. If available, the information is in state archives.

An example of a Bill of Sale issued after a slave purchase. Brown Brothers.

Tax Digests

The digest is an annual list of taxpayers, which records the amount and/or value of real and personal property, including land, residence, and the economic status of the slave master and of free blacks. It is possible to determine when a slave owner first acquired slaves and to trace the increase and decrease from year to year. If, for example, the tax digest does not record slaves for a known slave master until 1830, you can assume that prior to that time your ancestors had another owner.

If you cannot find a slaveholder in the census, try the tax digests for the county. It is also possible to track a slaveholder's movement. If the slaveholder paid taxes in one report and did not pay taxes in another, chances are he moved to a different area. Tax digests can also be found on microfilm at most state archives.

Church Records

Slaves—especially those in Catholic, Baptist, and Methodist communities, those in households with only a few domestic slaves, and those household slaves on large plantations—were often members of the local white church or allowed to practice the same religion as their slave master. Church records reflect admission, transfer, and dismissal of individuals and the administration of sacraments.

After the Revolutionary War, the white Methodists and Baptists began to recruit Negroes, who joined their organizations in large numbers. In the South, the lively revival meetings of these organizations attracted many slaves.

Remember the five-mile rule of thumb. Transportation was limited, so most people attended church within a five-mile radius of their home. Check the records of white churches in the area to see if they kept records of slave members.

During slavery, there were also a few black churches made up of free Negroes. As membership in white churches increased, it was not uncommon for separate Negro churches to be set up, particularly in the Eastern part of the United States. Richard Allen, founder of the Free African Society, the first black Methodist church, is one of the best-known free Negro preachers of this period. As this organization spread, the churches became known as African Methodist Episcopal Churches.

Former Africans stripped of their homeland rituals eventually embraced Christianity on a broad scale. Many Negro spirituals sung by slaves often reflected their deep abiding faith in God. They held hope for a better life after death, where they could "lay their burdens down" and "shout all over God's heaven." This is a belief still held by many African-Americans today.

The national headquarters for both the Baptist and Methodist churches are as follows:

National Baptist Convention, USA, Inc.
3455 Twenty-sixth Avenue South
St. Petersburg, FL 33711
813-328-1157

Christian Methodist Episcopal Church
4466 Elvis Presley Blvd.
Memphis, TN 38116
901-345-0580

Dr. Dennis E. Dickerson
Office of Historiographer
African Methodist Episcopal Church
P. O. Box 301
Williamstown, MA 01267
413-597-2484

Manumission Records

These were issued when a slaveholder granted a slave freedom. Records are held in county deed books and are sometimes attached to a slaveholder's will if he granted freedom to a slave upon the owner's death. The Pennsylvania Abolition Society and the Genealogy Society of Pennsylvania have thousands of manumission records on microfilm. The Schomburg Center for Research in New York City also has manumission records. The addresses for these institutions are listed in the Appendix.

Cemetery Records

Many private but basically church-affiliated cemeteries maintained records of interments. Slaves were buried in church-owned cemeteries, in family-maintained plots on the plantation, and in separate cemeteries reserved for blacks. Records may have been maintained by the cemetery owner.

These cemeteries are fairly easy to find if they still exist. The five-mile rule also applies here: slaves were generally buried within a five-mile radius of where they lived. If you go to the county courthouse and ask where the Negro cemeteries are, you are often directed to them. Sometimes, a genealogical society in the area has done a map or layout of who is buried there and where the body is located. But it is much more likely that you'll have to walk through each Negro cemetery, checking every headstone to find your ancestors.

Plantation Records

If you can find the plantation where your ancestors were enslaved, there may be annual records that the slave owner kept. Details about slaves sold, purchased, or runaways may be in these records. Lucky indeed is the genealogist who has these records as a source. Some plantation records have been donated to local genealogy libraries or state archives. A list of genealogy libraries is included in the Appendix.

Slave Narratives

One way to gain historical insight into the day-to-day life of a slave is to read slave narratives. These are actual writings or interviews with former slaves. These narratives can sometimes provide insight into what went on a plantation, and how the slave community interacted. One excellent collection is *The American Slave: A Composite Autobiography*. This 19-volume series includes narratives from Arkansas, Georgia, North Carolina, South Carolina, Alabama, Missouri, Indiana, Texas, Oklahoma, Kentucky, Tennessee, Virginia, Maryland, Ohio, Florida, and Mississippi. Most of these narratives are available at a public library.

Military Records

Free blacks and slaves performed military service in major wars. During the Revolutionary War and the War of 1812, slaves were sometimes given freedom in return for military service in many slave-holding states. Late in the Civil War, the Union Army admitted all-Negro units, which served valiantly. Military records generally include the serviceman's name, age, birthplace, residence, and occupation at enlistment. As amazingly complete as these records are, sometimes you have to dig deep to find an ancestor's military record, as one researcher discovered.

Frustrated, despondent, and ready to give up, genealogist Jeanette Braxton Secret feared she would never find out about her great-grandfather through military records. Growing up, she had heard stories from her aunt that her great-grandfather had fought in the Civil War. His family didn't know if he was part of the Union or the Confederacy. Jeanette assumed he was in the U.S. Colored Troops.

> *I had been searching three months with lots of back and forth communication with the [National] Archives, but no luck. I searched all 30 volumes of the official records of the War of the Rebellion for the Union and Confederate Army and Navy but found nothing. I even contacted the Library of Congress via mail to inquire about runaway slaves, contraband that may have served in Union but didn't find much information.*

Many slaves seeking freedom ran away during the Civil War and attached themselves to Union regiments. These runaway slaves were labeled "contraband" of war. Collection of the Library of Congress.

I discussed my disappointment with a friend who volunteered one night a week at the National Archives Regional Branch in San Bruno, California. He offered to search for me. The next day he called and said 'I found your great-grandfather, he served in the Navy.' He gave me the application number.

I called the [army] archivist back. To my surprise, it turns out she only knew about the Army and told me to call across the street to the Navy. I wish she had told me that in the beginning. I talked to the Navy archivist and she said, 'Oh yeah, he served and has a big file here.' It turns out the Navy was integrated during the Civil War. They did not have separate colored troops. They sent me a copy of my great-grandfather's file.

Jeanette learned that Iverson Granderson served in the Union Navy aboard four different ships: the USS *Great Western*, USS

Kickapoo, USS *Grand Gulf,* and the USS *Fearnot.* His rank was first-class boy or first-class colored boy. His job was a coal heaver. Naval ships operated on coal. He was injured in the battle of Mobile, Spanish Fort, which was a Confederate stronghold the Union captured to give it a strategic position in the South. The furnace door exploded while Granderson was heaving coal. The blast from the heat left him blind in one eye. He was discharged in 1865 in Brooklyn, New York.

To find out about the various battles Granderson fought in, and details about navy ships, Jeanette contacted the Naval Historical Center in Washington, D.C.

This is an example of information available in pension records. Pension files are often the most useful for genealogical research and contain the most information regarding a person's military career. According to National Archives documentation, "You should request copies of a military record only when no pension file exists."

Write the National Archives for copies of veterans' records prior to World War I. Records include those of the U.S. Army (officers who served before June 30, 1917, and enlisted men who served before October 31, 1912); the U.S. Navy (officers who served before 1903 and enlisted men who served before 1886); the Marine Corps (officers who served before 1896 and enlisted men who served before 1905); and the Confederate Armed Forces (officers and enlisted men who served from 1861 to 1865). Discharge certificates are not usually included as a part of a compiled military service record. Before 1944, Army regulations allowed the issuance of an original discharge certificate only, which was given to the soldier. Confederate soldiers in service at the time of surrender did not receive discharge certificates. They were give paroles, and these became their personal property. To obtain these records you need to fill out a copy of form NATF 80. There is a charge, and you will be billed if a record is found. You must fill out a separate request for each ancestor. Write to the following:

General Reference Branch (NNRG-P)
National Archives and Records Administration
Seventh Street and Pennsylvania Avenue NW
Washington, D.C. 20408

For records relating to service in World Wars I or II or earlier write to the Personnel Records Center. Records since World War II have not been released to the public. Do not use form NATF 80 as described above for these records. The address is:

National Personnel Records Center
(Military Records) NARA
9700 Page Boulevard
St. Louis, MO 63132

The key to research is persistence. Like Jeanette Braxton Secret, you also need faith that an oral history lead passed down for three or more generations probably has an element of truth at its core.

OTHER CHALLENGES: FEW WRITTEN RECORDS, NAME CHANGES, NICKNAMES, AND MIGRATION

You will encounter many such challenges during your research. Most slaves could neither read nor write, so no written legacy exists. Information on ancestors must be traced through the slaveholder's records and public records.

Slave women generally worked in the cotton fields from sunrise to sunset. Although dog-tired they often could not get a good night's sleep. White slave masters would periodically stroll down to the slave quarters under the cover of darkness and force these women into sexual liaisons. The practice was so common that many genealogists estimate that 90 percent of African-Americans have white ancestors in their family tree. That may not surprise you. But did you also know that 80 percent of you are just as likely to have a Native American ancestor in your family tree?

There was often a bond between African-Americans and Indians because of their shared persecution. Several Indian tribes were settled in slave-holding states. Many runaway slaves found a home among these Indian tribes. It was also common for African-Americans and Indians to marry. My Indian ancestors were Cherokee. If you'd like to research the Indian genes in your bloodline, begin with the National Bureau of Indian Affairs and the many books available on various tribes in libraries.

Slaves were generally given first names and took the last name of their slave owners. Many of these slaves were also given nicknames by their slave community or their masters. For example, one of my slave ancestors was named Virginia but was often listed in public records as Jenny. This problem is common on census records even after slavery. My grandfather was listed by his nickname, Bud, instead of his name, James, in one census report.

When slavery ended, many slaves dropped their former master's name and selected another. While some of these former slaves stayed on the farms as sharecroppers, many migrated to other parts of the country. Some black men, for example, became buffalo soldiers when they went west and joined the cavalry. Others just moved on to other plantation owners' land.

After slavery many sharecroppers were stuck in an endless cycle of poverty. They often heard of the promised land, referring to Northern cities like Chicago and Detroit. These cities had bustling factories that paid more in a month than sharecropping paid all year. Eventually there was a great migration of Southern blacks to these Northern cities.

The next chapter discusses resources for tracing African-American ancestors after the end of slavery.

OUT OF SLAVERY

Most slaves reacted with pure joy to the news of slavery's demise. After all, they had dreamed, prayed, and worked for this day. The Thirteenth Amendment ending slavery was signed into law in December 1865.

The transition to freedom was not easy, however, since most Southern whites could not adjust to a land where blacks were suddenly equal. Many whites resented the method of emancipation because they had suffered enormous loss of personal property and individual respect. But it wasn't just former slaveholders who were filled with resentment; as one reporter put it, "ex-nigger-drivers, ex-nigger-traders, ex-nigger-whippers and other representatives of the poor white community" were also unhappy. They simply could not accept Negroes as equals. Additionally, the Confederate currency was worthless at the end of the war and many Southern whites were penniless.

Because they owned their own land, my ancestors Ann, now a former slave, and her common-law husband Isaiah Parker Jr., a former slaveholder, were better off than many people following the Civil War. They rebuilt and lived out their lives on their land. Eight of their fifteen children had been born into slavery. The next seven were the first of the Parker branch of my family tree to be born free in the new United States. Seaborn was the first of Ann's children born free and the first of the black Parkers born free.

Isaiah Parker III and his family. Born in 1869, Isaiah was one of the fortunate last seven of Ann and Isaiah Parker Jr.'s fifteen children to be born free. Author collection.

Before Ann and Isaiah began to have children, all the Parkers had been white. When I think about how Ann must have felt giving birth to her son Seaborn, my eyes swell with tears: I can feel her joy.

POSTSLAVERY GENEALOGY RESOURCES

This chapter discusses genealogy resources available in the aftermath of the abolition of slavery.

A Note About Primary and Secondary Sources

There is a real problem in tracing African-American genealogy for the period between 1860 and 1870. This was a time of tremendous turmoil and upheaval in this country. People got lost in the written records, changed their names, and moved around. Begin your research with primary sources, such as census data, vital records, and cemetery and church records. After you have exhausted all primary sources, try using secondary sources, such as the Freedmen's Bureau records, sharecropping records, and the American Missionary Association records. If you are stuck and can't find your ancestors through primary sources prior to 1870, then these secondary-source records could be helpful and provide a good lead. Start with the information that pertains to the state you are researching. You must have patience when reviewing some of these records, which are handwritten and sometimes difficult to read.

Church Records

Yes, I'm mentioning church records again because they were just as important after slavery as they were during it. Once slavery ended, the newly freed slaves had no organized church structure or money to create ministries. Throughout the South there were no ministers to baptize Negro children, perform marriages, and bury the dead. Therefore, churches were established by those Negroes among the former slaves who had been "called to preach."

God may have called them but it was the African Methodist Episcopal Church or the National Baptist organizations that commissioned them. The Negro masses were concentrated in Methodist and Baptist churches. For this elite group, training preachers must have been quite a challenge since 95 percent of former slaves could neither read nor write.

The Gores were Baptist. My great-grandfather Elijah Gore and his brother Stanley were among the ministers in Georgia called to preach. They began preaching during Reconstruction following the Civil War. Many Southern counties had no permanent church building. As a result, many ministers like my great-grandfather established themselves as traveling ministers. On Sundays, they went from town to town preaching two or three times a day. Preaching was probably not a prosperous profession. People had very little money at the time. Many ministers were paid for their services with a sampling from parishioners' crops, pies or cakes, or with chickens from their farms.

My grandfather and four of his brothers followed in their father's footsteps and became ministers. If your ancestor was also "called to preach," searching Methodist and Baptist records may provide some excellent clues. Some suggested sources include the following:

- *Biographical Directory of Negro Ministers,* edited by Ethel L. Williams. This directory lists personal statistics such as family information, educational background, and church and religious affiliations.
- *Who's Who Among the Colored Baptists of the United States,* edited by Samuel Williams Bacote. This directory profiles several prominent early twentieth-century Baptist ministers.
- *The African Methodist Episcopal Zion Church: Reality of the Black Church,* by William J. Walls. This is available in public libraries.
- *Cyclopaedia of African Methodism,* by Alexander W. Wayman (Methodist Episcopal Book Depository, 1882). This is also available in public libraries.

Oral history claims my grandfather went to Morehouse College in Atlanta. In researching this information, I discovered that the Baptist Home Missionary Society was responsible for founding both Spelman and Morehouse colleges in Atlanta. Morehouse originated as a training school for teachers and preachers. It began as Augusta Institute in Augusta, Georgia, in 1867, and was unsuccessful. It was revived and moved to Atlanta as Morehouse College. Morehouse has records and yearbooks dating back to Reconstruction. These records may be helpful in tracing any ancestors who were preachers and attended Morehouse during Reconstruction. Unfortunately, I have not been able to find any Morehouse records to confirm my grandfather's attendance there as a student. He's not listed in any yearbooks.

There are other ways to utilize church records from the period after slavery. Genealogist Roland Barksdale Hall noticed the minister's name on his grandmother's death certificate. Using that name, he found the church his family attended. While the minister and his family members were deceased, he found eight church members who remembered his family well. Through oral interviews he got an understanding of when his family lived in that community and why they left it. Don't overlook church members and ministers as possible resources.

American Missionary Association

The American Missionary Association (AMA) was founded in 1846 and strove to bring about the abolition of slavery peaceably. The association believed that the U.S. Negro population should have the privileges of citizenship as outlined in the Declaration of Independence. This belief led the association to establish schools for Negroes in the South during the Civil War.

Runaway slaves flocked to the Union Army and were called "contraband." The first school was established by the AMA for Negro "contraband" at Fortress Monroe in Virginia in 1861. The AMA went on to develop over five hundred schools in the South. Additionally, the AMA founded Hampton University, Fisk University, and Atlanta University, and provided contributions and support to many other black colleges.

The Amistad Research Center located on the Fisk University campus is the depository for over 350,000 manuscripts of the association. The collection includes reports from missionaries, teachers, annual school reports, and letters. The papers are valuable as a resource for studying the abolitionist movement and the education of freedmen after the Civil War; there is also limited material on the Underground Railroad, letters from the association's missionaries about fugitive slaves in Canada, and biographies of some of the people of the movement.

This is a vast collection that has been put on microfilm. Begin with the three-volume index of the collection entitled, *Author and Added Entry Catalog of the American Missionary Association Archives*. It will give you some idea of where to begin. In addition to the Amistad Research Center, the collection can be found on microfilm in several libraries throughout the United States. See listing of libraries in the Appendix.

Sharecropping Records

Former slaves often worked someone else's land in exchange for a share of the crop, a practice which kept many blacks in perpetual debt and poverty. For sharecroppers, all food and clothing were purchased "on account," and when the crop came in, their debts were paid. Frequently no money was left and debts accumulated.

Sharecropping records are available in some local counties. These documents are often financially inaccurate because it was common practice to cheat. Since most newly freed slaves could neither read nor write they were at the mercy of the property owner for whom they worked to enter charges correctly. These records can, however, provide proof of an ancestor's residence. In addition, the National Archives has sharecropping records available to researchers.

Freedmen's Bureau

The Bureau of Refugees, Freedmen, and Abandoned Lands is generally referred to as the Freedmen's Bureau. This government agency was established in the War Department by an act of Congress in March 1865. Bureau responsibilities included supervision and management of all abandoned lands and control of all affairs relating to refugees and freedmen.

The bureau's services included providing assistance in obtaining employment through contracts with former slave owners; establishing schools; feeding, clothing, and obtaining medical treatment for freed slaves; locating separated family members; legalizing marriages; and investigating claims of brutality. The bureau also helped Negro soldiers and sailors file and collect claims for bounties, pensions, and back pay.

The basic management structure of the bureau included the assistant commissioner, the assistant adjunct general, and the assistant inspector general and some staff members. The collected documents were generally created or received by one of these people.

The Freedmen's Bureau's records are available on microfilm in national and state archives. The records consist of communications sent, registers and orders issued, unbound letters and reports received, and miscellaneous papers. Microfilm records are available for the following states: Alabama, Arkansas, Georgia, Louisiana, Mississippi, North Carolina, South Carolina, Tennessee, Texas, and Virginia, as well as the District of Columbia.

The records of the Education Division of the Bureau of Refugees, Freedman and Abandoned Lands are also available on microfilm in national and state archives and some libraries. The records consist mainly of letters, school reports, and pupil information. However, I did not find pupils listed by name in the reports I reviewed. The bureau worked with benevolent societies, such as the American Missionary Association, to establish schools.

The following are additional sources you may not have normally considered but that could be most helpful.

Freedmen's Saving and Trust Company
This was a federal bank system created to assist freed slaves and others in establishing a savings account. It was not affiliated with the Freedmen's Bureau. It existed from 1865 to 1874.

Twenty-nine branch banks were located in the District of Columbia and in all Southern states.

The company's noble mission was to encourage freedmen to save their money and invest in their own banks, creating a sense of personal pride. During that nine-year period, deposits from freedmen made the banks successful. Black churches and organizations also believed in and entrusted their money to the banks. The banks became community institutions. Eventually corruption and mismanagement caused the banks to fail, and the freedmen lost their meager savings. This scandal led to a long-held distrust of the banking system by blacks.

Useful genealogical information can be found in deposit ledgers and signature registers of the Freedmen's Saving and Trust Company. Some of the registers even contain personal family information, such as the name of a spouse, occupation, children's names, and beneficiaries. The amount of information varies per record.

The records are housed in the national and state archives and even some library genealogical collections. The following example is taken from an actual record to give you an idea of the information that can be found.

Record for: Joseph Jones
Date of application: Dec. 7. 1867
Age and complexion: 30/Black
Father: Thomas   **Mother:** Temby
Married: Nellie Jones
Name of children: Jerry, King, Mary
Regiment and Company:
Place of birth: Huntsville, Ala.
Occupation: Farmer
Remarks: Father died in 1862 Simestone, Mother lives with me. Has one brother Anthony-last hard (sic) from him in Misp. (sic)
Signature: Joseph X (his mark) Jones

Most of the freedmen did not know how to write, so many official documents were signed with an X as a person's mark.

A Town of Our Own

All-black communities were established and built in several states, including Oklahoma and Florida. Eatonville, Florida, one of the few towns still in existence, has a celebration once a year honoring its most famous resident, the late author Zora Neale Hurston.

Records of these towns can be found in state and local archives. If your ancestors are from these towns or grew up in nearby counties, these records are worth pursuing. Town documents may provide clues to information about residents, what life was like in the settlement, church records, and other useful genealogical information.

Negro Baseball League

The Negro Baseball League consisted of teams that played before baseball was integrated. Records for the Negro Baseball League are remarkably intact. Usually you can find out what year an ancestor played and at what position. Photographs of individual players and some teams are also available for a fee.

My uncle Jack Barry was a pitcher with the American Giants. My aunt Dolly said her older sister Melinda (Jack's wife) often took her and some of their younger sisters and brothers to watch him play.

Begin your search in directories that list Negro League ball players, which can be found in libraries and bookstores. The directories will help you find what team and year an ancestor played ball. Next, contact the Negro League Baseball Museum. At the time of this writing the museum was not open to the public. All requests for information must be in writing. When writing for information, include the player's name, team, and estimate of the year he played. Write to:

The Negro Leagues Baseball Museum
1601 East Eighteenth Street
Kansas City, MO 64108

Cowboys and Buffalo Soldiers

For information on life in the West, on specific cowboys, buffalo soldiers, people of achievement, and related information, write or visit:

Black American West Museum and Heritage Center
3091 California Street
Denver, CO 80205

Newspapers

Many black-owned newspapers from the period after Reconstruction were national papers. The *Chicago Defender, Pittsburgh Courier,* and *New York Age* were the most well known. Often these papers had reporters strategically located in numerous cities. So even if your community didn't have a black paper your ancestors could have been featured if they did something newsworthy.

The local general paper of your town or county is also a good source. Genealogist Roland Barksdale Hall's mother had given him a clipping from the *Sharon Herald* in Sharon, Pennsylvania. The article was about her grandfather, a former slave, who was celebrating his 109th birthday. Barksdale Hall said, "It was almost spiritual. I felt like she was passing down an important piece of family heritage. I felt she was telling me to preserve this fragile piece of paper."

Unfortunately, Barksdale Hall's article was not dated. So he found his great-grandfather's death certificate and discovered he had been born in November. From that the genealogist estimated the most probable year. He researched the November editions of the *Sharon Herald* for the three most likely years. He then read each paper for each November day of that three-year period. He found the article in a November 1949 edition.

Then Barksdale Hall got the idea to search national black papers and general papers from surrounding communities, including the *Youngstown Vindicator*. This was a popular big-city paper read by Sharon residents, published in Youngstown, Ohio. Barksdale Hall found this article in the *Vindicator*.

> *109 years old Sharonite born as slave in Georgia February 8, 1848. Mr. Stevenson is the only one of Pennsylvania's residents to be born in slavery. He is one of a family of 14 children born to Archie and Harriett in Newman, Georgia. His family being without a name adopted the name of their kind master.*

Although the paper got the birth month wrong, look at the gold mine of information in this one brief clipping: (1) the names of his great-great-grandparents; (2) the fact that they had fourteen children; (3) the information that the family was originally from Newman, Georgia; and (4) the surname of the slave owner. Now Barksdale Hall knew what town and under what surname to begin his census research, and what slave names he was trying to connect to the plantation.

THE GREAT MIGRATION

For black people, there was still a great deal of turmoil after the Civil War. There were good changes like the Freedmen's Bureau schools in which blacks were learning how to read. But there were still many dark days. Lynchings and beatings of predominantly black men in the South are legendary. Reasons did not have to be clear or proven in court. Things as minor as a police officer not liking your attitude, or smiling at a white woman, could have vicious consequences. As a result, many blacks left the South to get away from the brutality. Others left to save their necks.

An oral history story in my family recounts how my grandfather had an altercation early in the week when a white man said something about my grandmother that my grandfather didn't like. The following Sunday as my grandfather and his brother were coming home in the late evening from their preacher rounds they were stopped by several white men. They beat them and tied them to a tree and left them to die. That night it rained, and the brothers were able to free themselves from the wet ropes and make it back to their sharecropping farms.

My great-grandfather had already moved to Chicago. He wrote my grandfather about the opportunities in the steel factories and suggested he move North. Under the circumstances, my grandfather felt it was a good time to leave Georgia.

It was a common practice for relatives to go North and write home about the wonderful opportunities. The auto industry in Detroit and the steel industry and slaughterhouses in Chicago were examples of factories that offered wages many men could not make in the South. Additionally, the North had been glamorized both by relatives who were already living there and by the media. The *Chicago Defender* urged Southern blacks to come North to experience real citizenship. Black railroad porters would throw the weekly papers from the train so Southern blacks could read what was happening in Chicago.

Many blacks, tired of the poverty of sharecropping, decided to make the move. First small numbers but eventually thousands flocked to Northern cities. The black population of Chicago grew from 44,000 in 1910 to 109,000 in 1920 and then to 234,000 in 1930.

If any of your ancestors migrated North during this period, be sure to interview them soon to learn of their experiences firsthand.

Additionally, the *Chicago Defender* is still in operation, and is still one of the country's leading black newspapers. The old newspapers are on microfilm in several Chicago libraries and in some libraries in other cities. Read the papers for death notices or other family information that might be found in them. They are also a good resource for what was going on in the city and black community in the early 1900s.

The photo on page 21 is of my grandparents and several of their sixty-six grandchildren that ran in the *Defender* the year my grandparents celebrated the fortieth anniversary of my grandfather's church, Friendship Baptist. I am not in the photo; I hadn't been born yet. However, my brother Charles is the baby my grandfather is holding and my oldest brother Milton is standing in front of my grandmother.

There was also a lot of movement among blacks that had nothing to do with the great migration. "You have to trace the movement of your family," says genealogist Roland Barksdale Hall. "My family is from Georgia but I found an article that said my grandfather [was] employed as a steelman in Birmingham [Alabama]. . . . I checked the census and discovered he was a coal miner. From [the] 1890s to [the] 1930s they traveled to Birmingham to work in the coal mines to earn enough money to keep their farms going in Georgia. My grandfather's brother went to New Orleans to work on ships. One of my grandfather's sisters went to Massachusetts to teach. She saved her money and moved back to Georgia and bought a boarding house.

"People were more mobile than I had been led to believe," he continued. "The parents left the children to be raised by the grandparents in the security of the farm. I had wondered why I would find my great-grandparents with all these children. That was a strategy they used to survive back then."

An interesting recent trend shows African-Americans migrating back to the South. Several Southern cities like Atlanta, Charlotte, and Raleigh, North Carolina, are exploding in population growth.

Business and Professional Directories

Several African-American business and professional directories have been published since the late 1800s. The early directories can still be found in libraries with genealogical collections and those that specialize in black history.

PIECING TOGETHER YOUR HERITAGE

Tracing a person's genealogy is like fitting together the pieces of a puzzle. You take the bits of data you've researched, combine them with historical facts and oral history, and soon the puzzle of your family's heritage begins to take shape.

To piece together your heritage, be sure to combine information from a variety of sources. The census may help you discover your family lineage, while birth and death records provide details of age, parents' names, and cause of death. Military records or club affiliations can add dimension to your ancestors' life and photos preserve their likeness while adding visual interest to the project.

Put like information together from all sources—census, church records, and so on. One excellent example is the way genealogist Roland Barksdale Hall combined several elements to create his family's heritage. He took information from a little newspaper clipping, combined it with information from public records, and paired that with information from church records to develop some of the history of his family.

In my own experience, I used census records, probate court records, homestead court records, a book on local county history, and military records to piece together the story of the Parkers. Each record provides information that adds details and facts that eventually combine to create your family's story.

One of my favorite quotes on the importance of understanding our past as we mold our future was written by Martin Luther King Jr. He said, "The Negro must always guard against the danger of becoming ashamed of himself and his past. There is much in the heritage of the Negro that each of us can be proud of. The oppression that we have faced, partly because of the color of our skin, must not cause us to feel everything non-white is objectionable. The content of one's character is the important thing, not the color of the skin. We must teach every Negro child that rejection of heritage means loss of cultural roots, and [that] people who have no past have no future." (From the November 1957 issue of *Ebony* magazine.)

Whenever I tell people I'm a genealogist, they ask two questions: how far back can you go and can you trace your family to Africa? No book on African-American genealogy would be complete without a discussion on our African heritage and how to trace your genealogy to Africa. The next chapter will provide some basic information and guidelines.

THE AFRICAN CONNECTION

Our African-American history did not begin in slavery but among family and neighbors in an African village. We are proud descendants of a cultured and noble people. To date, I cannot trace exactly where my forefathers, the Gores, were captured and stolen from their homeland or where they boarded the ship for the perilous journey to America. In all probability they were ripped from their homeland in West Africa.

In some cases, the dungeons of Elmina Castle on the Gold Coast (now the independent nation of Ghana) were the slaves' last stop in Africa. Elmina (meaning the mine) was a slave detention depot—a castle port used by the Portuguese to serve the European-African gold and spice trade. Located on the waterfront of the Atlantic Ocean in Ghana, Elmina became a slave dungeon. It was easily accessible to anchored ships.

Millions of captured Africans, Mandinkas, Fulas, and Walofs passed through the Maison des Esclaves, or house of slaves. There were quarters upstairs for merchants and traders. Captured slaves were held in the castle's dark, airless dungeon chained to the walls with manacles. The castle's courtyard was the place where slaves were branded. They were held under these conditions until the ship waiting offshore reached its quota of cargo.

Forty-five such forts were built on the Gold Coast alone. Other well-known slave forts include Cape Coast Castle,

Christianborg, Goree Island, and Fort Metall Cross. Captured slaves, always in coffles and yokes, were placed in these forts, which served as temporary slave prisons.

In 1994, I made a pilgrimage to Africa with the family of Alex Haley. The trip was coordinated by William (Bill) Haley (Alex's son), whose company, the Haley Travel Service, encourages pilgrimages by African-Americans to Africa. The ten-day trip took us to Senegal and Gambia. We visited the slave fort on Goree Island and the village of Juffureh, Kunta Kinte's home village, made famous in Alex Haley's book *Roots*. Upon landing, Africans greeted us with "Welcome home, sister," and "Welcome home, brother." I experienced an incredible feeling of joy to be in the motherland, the place where my family was born, and where my deepest roots lay. It was an important time in my genealogy quest.

In Juffureh we were welcomed by the village leaders. The village was much the same as it was hundreds of years ago before Kunta Kinte was captured. The thatched roof huts are designed so they absorb the sun's heat in order to warm the hut at night. Extended families generally live together, and each member contributes to the well-being of the entire family.

The village griot gave us African names. My given name is *Binta,* a name often given to the firstborn girl of a family in the Mandinkas tribe.

Although I cannot pinpoint where my ancestors came from in Africa, this experience still gave me a family connection and a sense of what typical village life would have been for my family. To give us a place to call home, we were each given honorary membership in the family of Kinte.

THE BUSINESS OF SLAVERY

Our visit to Goree Island was like stepping back in time. The slave fort was built in 1776 by the Dutch, the first white people in West Africa. At that time, it was the most important slave transit center in West Africa. Here, 150 to 250 Africans would be held for up to three months.

Upon arriving at the fort, Africans were immediately split up with holding rooms for men, women, and children, who were taken from their mothers. Captives who were not big enough were put in a special room for fattening in order to fetch a better price. Their names were taken and they were given numbers. The worth of a man was determined by his teeth and muscles; the woman by her teeth and breast size.

The dungeons in which the slaves were shackled at the wrists and ankles were appallingly small; between forty and fifty people were packed in a space large enough for only twenty. The hole where disruptive or seemingly unruly Africans were held in solitary confinement was not large enough for me, a very short person, to stand erect. Average-sized persons would have had to curl up to fit into this stone container. There were no windows in any dungeon areas. The holding chambers were still dark and spooky even though the bars had been removed.

I can only imagine the terror that filled the minds and hearts of Africans kidnapped from their homeland. Entire families were split up: the father could be sent to Louisiana; the mother to Brazil or Cuba; and the children to the Caribbean. All fifty of my traveling companions were moved by the experience. Tears flowed down cheeks, people held hands, some hugged, and we all prayed. I was so moved by the visit to Goree Island, that I immediately wrote the following poem.

Speak, Mother Africa

Speak to me mother Africa,
let your drumbeat roar.
Tell me of the children
stolen from your shore.

Listen to me child and
hear the cries from my soul.
They beat them and shackled them
the pain and sorrow goes untold.

Stripped from their families,
villages, communities and homes.
They stole the blood of Africa
and the strength within her bones.

Slavers and slave ships
waiting off my shores
Captured mighty Africans
calling them black gold.

They sailed from my shores
while all their hopes burned.
Leaving from slave forts like
Goree Island's door of no return.

Mandinkas, Fulas, Walofs
were names of their tribes.
Many never made it to the
West Indies or America alive.

As you return to your homeland
my child, do not cry for me.
Just remember the past,
make the present better and
know that Africa is
rising to the future!

The demand for slave labor in the New World led to a highly organized trade in Africa that was supplied by peaceful means of purchase or outright warfare and raids. A sad truth is that whites alone did not build the successful slave business. They were helped by many Africans who captured their fellow countrymen during tribal wars and sold the prisoners to slave traders out of greed or for economic survival. These Africans also worked as guides for slave traders.

Slaves were brought to the New World in specially built ships that could carry large cargoes. Ships were literally packed with human cargo; four to six hundred tightly packed slaves in the bowels of the ships with no room except on the top deck. Here is where the slaves were exercised in chains and once per day doused with seawater. Below the top deck there was only crawling room.

How the Slave Trade Affects Your Search

Many genealogists wish we could, hope we can, and try every avenue possible to find our African roots. The truth is most of us will never be able to connect to an African ancestor or to his or her tribe.

There are a few, however, who have a lead passed down from their family. This is how Alex Haley found Kunta Kinte. Other genealogists discover a legal document, such as a bill of sale, that points the way to an African village or tribe. If you are so blessed, the following are things you can do to search out your African heritage.

FINDING YOUR WAY TO YOUR AFRICAN HOMELAND

"I think every African-American should visit Africa," encourages Bill Haley. "I feel a pilgrimage is something spiritual, an opportunity to reconnect to our African roots. Most people can't connect to Africa until they go there. They don't feel good because Africa has been dehumanized. A pilgrimage gives you a sense of personal history and adds clarity to the phrase, 'so this is where they brought us from.'"

I can attest to that spiritual connection Haley referred too. A trip to a slave fort like Goree Island will give you a sense of connection to your African ancestor even if you never know his or her name or ethnic group.

To begin the search for your African connection, start with a review of the oral histories you've collected. Were there any clues to your African heritage, such as the name of a tribe, country, or an African name passed down through the generations? If so, begin with that clue. If, for example, you know what African country your ancestors came from, try to find the records of slave ships that sailed from the closest port.

Slave Ships

The records of the Lloyd's of London insurance company are the best source of information on slave ships. This company was responsible for insuring the shipping companies and their cargo. In these records you may find which port a ship picked up cargo from, the ship's name, the port it sailed from (its home port), and the captain's name. The company also published its own newspaper, the *Lloyd's List*. The paper tracked each ship's movement through various ports from 1740 to 1826.

Bill Haley, an expert on how to search for your African ancestry, states, "The business of slavery was no arbitrary business. Not everyone was in this business. Only one or two trading companies came into a specific port. They may have had twenty shipping stops but they generally returned to those same places consistently. Remember your history. Prior to 1780 America was a British colony, so slave ships to America were actually British ships."

You can find Lloyd's of London insurance records at the National Archives in Washington.

Also, check for ship records at maritime museums. Perhaps local historical societies can also be useful.

Maritime Museums
Naval Historical Center
Dept. of Navy
Operational Archives Branch
Washington Navy Yard
901 M Street Southeast
Washington, D.C. 20374

Navy Pier Maritime Museum
600 E. Grand
Chicago, IL 60602

The National Archives in Washington, D.C. also has maritime records related to the United States such as Coast Guard, Bureau of Customs, Maritime Bureau of Navigation and more.

If a slave owner purchased slaves at an auction, there may be a bill of sale listing the ship the slave arrived on. Check for these property deed records at state archives.

Ports of Entry

If you have no clues as to what ship your ancestors may have sailed on, but know the plantation where your ancestors served, start with the closest port of entry. According to Haley, prospective slave buyers generally picked ports that were no more than a week's journey from their farms, because slaves were chained and had to walk.

The primary ports were New York; Newport, Rhode Island; Boston; Baltimore; Philadelphia; Roanoke, Virginia; and Savannah, Georgia. Contact maritime museums, the Port Authority, and state archives for records on ships that came in and out of their ports, and for details on the various kinds of ships.

Additional resources include maritime museums, long-standing insurance companies that insured slave ships, and ships' logs. Look for these records at the National Archives also.

TRAVELING TO AFRICA
Family Name and Ethnic Group

"There are several facets to consider when researching in Africa," says Haley. "First, in Africa, family name is the key. Certain names—Kinte, Gayes, Diob—were family names belonging to certain ethnic groups. If your research has turned up a family name, you'll have an easier time finding your ethnic group.

"Secondly, 90 percent of Africans who were delivered to America during the slave trade came from the west coast of Africa. Those from other regions in Africa, usually went to other parts of the world. So beginning your search in West African countries like Senegal, Gambia, Ghana, Guinea, and the Ivory Coast is a practical choice. Many Africans can look at you and tell you what people group you're from. That's important because people groups are all related. Of course this visual method is a lot less quantifiable but it's a start."

"Knowing your ethnic group is important because it will give you a location on which to focus and you can try to discover some insight on various villages. Have you heard the popular African proverb, 'It takes a whole village to raise a child'? It's easy to do that in Africa because a village is a family compound. Everyone in the village is related by blood or marriage. The village is named for the family that occupies it."

Visual cues can give you insight to your ethnic group. Even across the ocean and after more than a hundred years, certain ethnic groups have the same gait, body language, and smile. Haley says, "If someone has said of you, 'She walks just like her daddy,' you probably also walk like your granddaddy, great-granddaddy, and your African ancestor. If the people look like, walk like, talk like your folks, if you can feel kinship, you may be on to something."

The Oral Tradition

Another important dimension in African research is the oral tradition. The oral tradition is older than the written tradition. It is strong and tends to be event-focused. If you can find a family name, locate a griot and see if he can help. Many European anthropologists have written down the history told to them by griots. This information is available in the national archives of various West African countries.

Where will you find a griot or locate a country's archives? Begin with that country's U.S. embassy. Most embassies are located in Washington, D.C. Ask the diplomatic liaison where he recommends you begin your research in his country.

I contacted the Permanent Mission of Gambia in Washington, D.C. A friendly, knowledgeable diplomat recommended three sources: the Gambia National Archives and the Gambia National Library, both located in the city of Banjul, and a local historian, whose name and telephone number he gave me.

If you visit Africa consider working with a local historian. A local historian can provide you with cultural background, help you find a griot, and put Africa's history in focus for you. You should be prepared to pay for these consulting services. Currency varies in each country, but ten to twenty dollars per hour, based on U.S. currency, seems fair. Or you can work out a flat rate for full-day service. But rates should be negotiated based on the kind of service and details involved. A listing of African archives, libraries, and museums can be found in the Appendix section of this book.

There are also U.S. embassies in African countries. Correspondence with them may provide some useful information as well. A listing of West African embassies in the United States and U.S. Embassies in Africa can also be found in this book's Appendix section.

Have Realistic Expectations

After the trip to Africa, Bill Haley gave me two special gifts from his family's archives. One was an autographed copy of *Roots* and the other was a set of copies of letters Alex Haley wrote his family from all over the world while he was researching his book. In one of his letters, dated June 16, 1967, Alex said the following about *Roots*:

"It's a first-of-its-kind book, that will set a most important new precedent. No Negro family ever has been able to trace itself this far back. I consider the African material is, in its way, little short of epochal—don't you? In a way, though it's our family, actually it's the story of every Negro in America (or Brazil, or the West Indies). As I say somewhere in the text, only the slaver ships and the surnames would be different."

If you cannot trace your family back to Africa, don't be disappointed. Know that our story was wonderfully and beautifully told in the book *Roots,* by the grandfather of African-American genealogy, Alex Haley.

Now that you've begun to collect your data you'll need to organize it and keep up with the details. The next chapter takes a look at how to write and publish your genealogy.

WRITING AND PUBLISHING YOUR FINDINGS

Genealogy can be a lifelong pursuit. At some point, however, genealogists must stop researching long enough to publish their findings. Publishing your work and sharing it with other family members is the perfect culmination of years of research that will be read by present and future descendants. Publishing prevents all the hard work and costly research from being destroyed or lost. It also prevents your relatives from needlessly researching information you have already obtained.

Self-publishing is stimulating, demanding, and rewarding. You'll have to wear many hats. In essence, you are the producer, director, marketer, and salesperson of this production. Don't feel that this task is beyond you. There is plenty of help available to assist you in bringing your project to life. You don't have to personally do every part of the project. You do, however, have to select and supervise those you hire or convince to help you. You are ultimately responsible for the success of the final work.

WHEN TO PUBLISH YOUR FINDINGS

My fifteen years of research had failed to turned up the slave owner or the plantation on which the Gores lived. This had left a gaping hole in the research for the Gore side of my family tree. I had been reluctant to publish because I felt my family's history was incomplete without this information. Additionally, the Gores were to be my primary customer base for selling the book, and I knew they'd want to know these important details.

An oral history lead I had previously overlooked sparked a connection that led me to the missing information (see Chapter 2). Once I determined the plantation on which the Gores had been slaves, I decided to publish my findings. At that point I felt I had enough information on both the Parkers and the Gores to provide my family a thorough historical narrative about our family's heritage. It was time to share the information I had discovered about which my family knew nothing.

When and what to publish is an individual decision each genealogist must make. Some people publish after they've researched as far back as they can go. Other researchers take on the project for a year and publish their discoveries in time for a specific family reunion, and then provide updated revisions at subsequent reunions. Still others just publish an individual ancestor's oral history. Basically, the most suitable publishing point is when you've got enough information to give your family some insight into the family's genealogy and heritage. And if my family members could give you an encouraging suggestion, they'd say, "Don't take fifteen years like Donna did!"

You don't have to wait until you've unearthed every detail, interviewed each and every relative, and followed every lead. After all, that could take a lifetime. Remember you can update and revise in later years if you discover more information.

PRESENTING YOUR FINDINGS

The biggest challenge is determining what is the best way to present the information. Will your book be a listing of ancestors by generation? Will it include all your family lines or just a few? Will you tell a story or just write down the facts? Should you include your oral interviews separately or incorporate them in the story? Will it be a pictorial with brief descriptions or will you incorporate photographs to highlight your story? More than likely you will use a combination of all of the above. Let's review three popular techniques.

Descendant Listing Format

This format is simply a complete listing of the names in a family genealogy. Often these genealogies trace back to the immigrant ancestor. The Bible is a good example of this style of genealogy (from I Chronicles 1:34–37).

> *And Abraham begot Isaac. The sons of Isaac were Esau and Israel.*
> *The sons of Esau were Eliphaz, Reuel, Jeush, Jaalam and Korah.*
> *And the sons of Eliphaz were Teman, Omar, Zephi, Gatam and Kenaz and by Timna, Amalek.*
> *The sons of Reuel were Nahath, Zerah, Shammah, and Missah.*

Many genealogy publications are boring, with long lists of dates and names. While this method may provide an accurate lineage, it provides no insight into the life and times of the people mentioned. As I've been preaching in this book, this should not be your chosen method. You want your book to spark interest in your family's story.

Biographical Format

This method tells your family's story in narrative form. It is a recommended format. Tell your family's story in plain, simple language.

Begin by writing a biography of the earliest known ancestor. Biographies of this ancestor, his or her spouse, and their children will be Chapter 1. Biographies of the ancestor's grandchildren

The wedding of my parents, Lindsey Smith and Helen (Gore) Smith, in 1945. My mother was the first in her family to have a formal wedding. When you are researching your family heritage, collect as many old photographs and documents as you can to help bring your family's story to life. Author collection.

could make up Chapter 2, the great-grandchildren Chapter 3, and so on. In this method each generation has its own chapter. Within these chapters you should include anecdotes, tall tales, and photographs.

I think a brief historical discussion on what was going on in the country should be included. This discussion adds interest.

Assuming you've done your ancestor charts and family group sheets, you're ready for the next step: writing a biography of each ancestor. Write this in paragraph form. Put the person's name and number at the top. Write down all the information you have collected about this ancestor. Pick up all the data and locate information from your ancestor's chart and family group sheet.

This is the time to include all the other information you've collected.

Include both the important and the trivial. You never know; that trivial bit of information may some day springboard you to a great discovery. It's your choice. You are the researcher, and you decide what to include and what to eliminate. Note the sources of your information. The following are a couple of examples of a family biographical sketch.

NUMBER 14—JULIUS PARKER

Julius Parker was born in July 1851 in Harris County, Georgia. He was the eldest son of Isaiah and Ann Parker's 15 children. He was born a slave. His father was a white man, the son of the slaveholder, who was also named Isaiah. His mother was a mulatto slave on the plantation. He was 14 when slavery ended. He married Alice Upshaw whose father was African-American and whose mother was believed to be a Cherokee Indian. They had 12 children: Julius Jr., Herschel, Fletcher, Ann, Daisy, Isaiah, Sanford, Florence, Virgil, Hattie, Toby, and Elizabeth. He eventually moved to Chicago. (Sources: 1850 and 1860 Census, oral history)

NUMBER 2—LINDSEY SMITH

Lindsey Smith was the second son of Lindsey Sr. and Georgia Robinson (Smith). He was born on December 3, 1916, in Mobile, Alabama. His nickname was Coot. He had two brothers, William and Charles, and two sisters, Virginia and Margarite. His family moved to Philadelphia briefly but eventually settled in Chicago. Lindsey went to Doolittle Elementary School and Phillips High School.

He loved the military and joined the Illinois militia as soon as he became of age. When World War II broke out his unit was called into active duty. He was a communications officer for the U.S. Army's 184th Field Artillery. This was an all-Negro unit. He served with distinction for five years and saw action in Europe. After the war Lindsey went to work for Western Electric in Chicago as a machinist and stayed there 35 years until his retirement.

continues

> *continued*
>
> He married Helen Gore on September 29, 1945, and they had four children, Milton, Charles, Donna and Michael. He was a devoted family man who loved weekend family get-togethers. He had no hobbies but was a fun guy and loved to party. Every accomplishment in the family was a reason to celebrate.
>
> He died in his sleep of heart disease at age 68 on January 18, 1985, and is buried at Lincoln Cemetery in Chicago. (Sources: marriage license, military discharge papers, death certificate, oral history, personal knowledge)

Some biographies will be more interesting than others. For some people you will have a lot of information and on others only a line or two. Just include what you have. If you find out more information, you can always add it later. If you have photographs of the ancestor, include them with the biographies.

Story Format

Using this method tells the family history as a story, and includes elements from the descendant listing and biographical formats. In the story format, family history, descendant lineage, and U.S. historical facts are blended together to tell the family heritage. This is the method I used in my family's genealogy. This format is great to use if you have a lot of information, can weave it together so it flows logically, and can write it so it is easy to understand. The following is taken from my family's genealogy book and is representative of the story format. It is excerpted from Chapter 4, "The Estate."

> Like everyone else in the South, the Parker family was gearing up for a possible war. They didn't have long to wait. In April 1861 the attack on Fort Sumter in South Carolina was the spark for the great conflict that exploded upon the land.
>
> *continues*

continued

Isaiah Parker Sr., as a rich slaveholder with both his land and his "right to own slaves" to protect, was no doubt in favor of the Confederacy. He probably encouraged his sons to defend their family, their land, and the great state of Georgia. Isaiah Sr., however, would never see or experience the hardships of the Civil War.

That same April the country went to war, the Parkers had a devastation of another kind. Isaiah Parker Sr. died suddenly. Adding to the loss and confusion, he failed to leave a will. While the state rapidly mobilized for war, the Parkers mobilized to take on the probate court.

The Parker brothers, Fleming and Isaiah, had to go to court to fight for their right as next-of-kin to be executors of the estate. Mahaley, Isaiah Sr.'s wife, was not mentioned in any of the court records. She was probably already deceased. The sons had to put up a bond for $50,000, which represented twice the amount of the estate. The court ordered a full appraisal of the estate of "Isaiah Parker Sr." by appraisers Andrew Huling & James Sterling.

The spring of 1861 was a dark time for Parker slaves. The appraisers came out to the plantation and probably lined the slaves up like the horses and the mules. To determine the value of each slave they would have looked at their teeth, measured their height, asked their age, and felt the muscles in their arms and legs. Then each slave was assigned a value. For Ann and her children this had to be one of the most humiliating days in her life as a slave. Imagine Isaiah having to explain to Ann the appraisal was necessary to determine each slave's value because the slaves, including Ann and their children, were to be sold like the land. I'm sure he assured her he would do all he could to purchase her and their children but there were no guarantees.

Having to deal with the probate court was rough for the Parkers I'm sure. But for me as a genealogist, it was a fantastic piece of luck. Because the court ordered a complete appraisal, every slave was listed and valued. It was easy to find the names of my family on the appraiser's inventory report.

Ann $1500	Julius $600
John Henry $1000	James Peter $400
Virginia (Jenny) $800	Hiram $200

continues

continued

Master Parker's estate included 900 acres of land more or less; 24 slaves; 4 mules; 4 horses; 89 hogs; 26 head of cattle; 2 oxen; 3,000 feet of lumber; 10 guns; plow tools; farm tools; a crop cut saw; axes; 1 buggy; 1 wagon; furniture; meat; lard; 249 bushels of wheat; 250 bushels of corn; 10,000 pounds of oats; and 4 promissory notes. Total appraised value of the estate was $35,340.

The probate court on June 3, 1861, granted Isaiah Jr. and Fleming the right to be the executors of the estate, first to settle his debts and then to pay over to his legal heirs the balance of the estate. Fleming and Isaiah had to keep the $50,000 bond posted until the estate was settled.

The land was sold among the heirs on Dec. 3 as follows:

200 acres	Sanford	$ 787
213 acres	John	$1040
225 acres	Fleming	$1384
152 acres	Isaiah	$1163
152 acres	Elizabeth	$1163
Total 942 acres		$5537

Each heir paid half cash and half over 12 months with no interest.

The Parker plantation was now five Parker farms and life would never be the same. While the turmoil of dividing the estate was winding down for the Parker family, the trouble for the slaves was still to come.

January 8, 1862, finally arrived. This was the day the slaves had surely waited and feared. It was the day they would be sold at auction. Each of the white Parker children had first claim and an equal right to purchase the slaves. Cousin Karen reports an oral history story that says, when the slaves were being auctioned after his father's death, Isaiah had a friend come to the auction. Whenever one of his siblings or anyone else would bid, the friend would say a dollar more and that's how he was able to keep so many of them together.

For Ann, the sale did not go as she'd probably prayed. Ann and her children, John Henry, Peter, Hiram, and an infant were sold to Isaiah Parker. But two of Ann's little ones would not be coming home that night. Virginia (Jenny) and Julius were sold to Elizabeth Parker Satterwhite, Isaiah's sister. Splitting up the family must have been incredibly painful for Ann. Virginia was only 8 years old and Julius was just 10. They still needed their mother."

In the story format there is still a chapter for each generation, but there may also be chapters that set the historical stage on which the family's history is played out. For example, in my family's book I have a chapter on the Civil War and the contribution the Parker family made to the war.

Chapters do not have to be ten pages long or any other specific length. Some of my chapters are only two or three pages. It depends on how much information you have on a particular generation or subject matter.

Publishing your family's story is a challenging undertaking no matter what format you use. But it can also be immensely rewarding. Try to give your work some pizzazz. Be generous with photographs and personal anecdotes. Share some tall tales from the oral histories you've collected. The following are suggestions for managing the job.

PREPARE A MANUSCRIPT OUTLINE

This is the most important step in writing your family history. Without an outline, you are apt to wander from family to family and generation to generation. The book outline should be in sufficient detail that it becomes a table of contents for the book. A sample table of contents is shown later in this section.

The most common way to present the data is to begin your book with your earliest known ancestors and work down to the present generation. Once you've selected your format, organize your data in file folders by chapter. Then you can start to write the draft manuscript.

I chose to divide my family's genealogy book into two parts. The first part is my family history told in the story format. In other words, it's told from my point of view. I described the action and historical events as I discovered them. I tried to place the information in historical context so that people would have some understanding of what was going on in the country at the time. The first part of the book covered my family's history from

1790 to 1900; or put another way, from my earliest known ancestor through the marriage of my grandparents, James and Annie, in 1902.

The second part of my book is the oral history. I decided to transcribe the interviews exactly as my aunts and uncles told them to me. I felt it was the safest way. I did not want any of my sixty-six first cousins tracking me down and saying, "Why did you say that about my mother or father?" This was information my aunts and uncles gave me permission to tell. So I let each of them tell their own story in their own voice. It is a wonderful snapshot into their lives.

The following is the table of contents from the book I wrote on my family's genealogy. It includes a brief description of what is in each chapter.

FAMILY PRIDE: THE STORY OF THE PARKERS AND THE GORES (1790–1970)

Acknowledgments   Here I thanked those who helped with the book and the research.

Foreword   This was written by Bill Haley, Alex's son. The Foreword discusses the need to preserve African-American family legacies to pass down to future generations.

Part One—The Family History

Introduction   This is a personal reflection about my research.

Chapter 1: African Homeland   This chapter discusses my trip to Africa and what is known about my family's African heritage.

Chapter 2: Setting the Historical Stage   This chapter describes what was happening in Georgia in the 1860s.

Chapter 3: The Parker Plantation   This chapter discusses the plantation where my ancestors were slaves.

Chapter 4: The Estate   This chapter details what happened when the plantation owner died without a will and how his death affected the slave families.

Chapter 5: The Civil War   This chapter is about the Civil War and the role the Parker family played in it, including the death blow it dealt slavery.

Chapter 6: Julius and Alice   This chapter is devoted to my great-grandparents. It tells of their life after slavery. Julius was the son of Isaiah Parker Jr. and his wife Ann. Julius was born a slave in 1851.

Chapter 7: The Gores   This is the family history of the Gores, my mother's father's family.

Chapter 8: James and Annie   This chapter is devoted to the marriage and life of my grandparents, who had twenty children, including my mother Helen.

Family tree charts   There are two charts. One shows the Parker and Gore genealogy. The other shows James and Annie (my grandparents), their twenty children, and their sixty-six grandchildren.

Part Two—Oral History and Family Photos

This second part includes the oral interviews plus photographs of my aunts and uncles and their families. Each chapter is named for the featured relative, that is, the one who was interviewed.

Anna Mae	Julius	Benjamin	Helen
Bernice	Mary	Melinda	Louise
Elijah	James Jr.	Minnie	Lorenzo
Hazel	Margaret	Richard	Florence

The Writing Process

Begin your book with an introduction; it will warm you up and get your creative juices flowing. The introduction can discuss why you're writing the book, give some highlights of your research, and/or discuss relatives you may not have met had you not taken on this project. Next, take out the folder for Chapter 1 and begin writing. Go to Chapter 2, and so on. Don't think of it as writing a book, rather think of it as writing a chapter. Remember, it is just a string of chapters that make a book.

Remember that writing a book takes time. If you are working toward a goal like a family reunion, be sure to begin months in advance. You may need to start a year ahead depending on how much time you have each week to sit down and write. Your research and your written words are a gift to your family and to

African-American history. Your family was here, and it left a mark. You are recording memories for generations to come. It is your contribution to the story of a people.

USE PHOTOGRAPHS GENEROUSLY

Don't you just love old photographs? Taking the trip down memory lane to see your mother and father when they were young or seeing your siblings as kids is still a fun way to spend an evening. Photographs provide a link to our past. Whether displayed or mounted in albums, these images are pegs for memories and sources of family history. As a genealogical researcher, you'll find collecting family photographs that help preserve the family's visual heritage to be a joyous part of your job.

My photo collection dates back to the late 1800s. Since photo styles varied during different historical periods, photographs can help estimate a relative's age range by the type of photography used. For example, my grandfather had a brother named Stanley, who was a preacher. I had two pictures that I thought were of Reverend Stanley Gore. They didn't actually look like the same person but an age gap of twenty or thirty years can make a man look different. As I collected more photographs I realized the photographic methods used to produce the two pictures were from two totally different historical periods. Therefore, the pictures could not possibly be of the same man.

This sent me back to my family pedigree charts. I realized that the Stanley in the older photo was my great-grandfather's brother Stanley. It turned out that my great-grandfather had named one of his sons after his brother, a common practice. The elder Stanley had been five years old when freedom was given to the slaves.

Try to collect black-and-white photos whenever possible. These can last for over a hundred years. Color photos have a life span of about fifty years. This means the color snapshots your

REV. S. C. GORE, D. D.

Pastor of the Providence Baptist Church
Putnam County, Geoegia
Colporter of the National Baptist Publishing Board
Nashville, Tenn.

Stanley Gore (Elijah Sr's. brother)

Reverend Stanley Gore, Doctor of Divinity (D.D.), was five years old when freedom was granted to the slaves. This is an example of postcard photography that was popular in the early 1900s. Author collection.

parents have taken of you may not outlast the black-and-white pictures taken of them. When you take photographs of family history, at a family reunion, for example, don't just take color shots. Take a roll of black-and-white film as well. The pictures will last longer.

Another suggestion from genealogists is to record more than just the name about a photograph. Include a little family history or a personal reflection with each photo. This will create a more interesting family album.

Photographs Require Special Care

Photos are a historic resource and need proper care and storage. Changes in temperature, dust, direct sunlight, and humidity are harmful and can make images deteriorate prematurely. The following information on the care of your photo collection was provided by Diane Ryan, Acting Curator of Prints and Photography at the Chicago Historical Society.

Handling and Organization

Handle a photograph by its edges with clean hands, or use cotton or nylon gloves to avoid depositing harmful skin oils on images.

Remove paper clips, staples, and rubber bands. Avoid using Post-It–type notes with photographs. They may leave indentations, rust, and other harmful chemical residues.

Use a soft lead pencil (such as Ebony brand pencils) and write close to the edges when marking your photographs. Write on a hard surface to avoid impressions in the emulsion.

Display

Do not use photo albums you can purchase in discount stores to store your family's photo history, particularly the "magnetic" type with peel back adhesive sheets. While they are reasonably priced, they may actually be harmful to your photos. Often the

This photograph of Margaret Crawford, my father's distant cousin, is the oldest in my collection. I estimate it was taken in the late 1890s or early 1900s. Old photographs need special care for preservation as discussed in this chapter. Author collection.

plastic holders are made of polyvinyl chloride and may make photos fade and discolor over time. Also the sticky backing may bond to the back of the photo and cause deterioration. The best and safest route is to use high-quality, photo-safe albums with sleeves that use acid-free paper.

Avoid adhesives that directly contact photographs. Use photo mounting corners or hinges made from polyester or acid-free paper. Framed photographs should be protected with glass or Plexiglas. The glass in a frame should not touch the surface of a photograph. Provide an overmat to guard against the glass adhering to the emulsion in humid conditions.

Supply Stores

Photo-safe albums can be purchased at art supply stores. You can also order them by direct mail from the following two sources.

Light Impressions
439 Monroe Avenue
P.O. Box 940
Rochester, NY 14603
(800) 828-9859

Gaylord Bros.
P.O. Box 4901
Syracuse, NY 13221
Phone: (800)428-9859

You can expect to pay about forty dollars for these 10 × 13 inch albums. They will, however, protect your photographs for generations to come.

Storage

When storing photographs choose a location that has a stable temperature and humidity and protect your collection from light. Do not store photographs in wood drawers, in boxes, or on wood shelves. Baked enamel on steel, such as that used to make filing cabinets, is the preferred material for drawers and shelves. Do not store newspaper clippings and other important papers with photographs. Do not laminate important documents or treasured keepsakes. The chemical process used in lamination accelerates the chemical aging of documents and other paper items.

HOW TO GENERATE INTEREST IN YOUR BOOK

Use a lot of photographs. There will be many relatives who will never read your book who will buy it just to look at the pictures of their relatives and ancestors.

Brag about your ancestors where appropriate. Mention unique talents, honorable deeds, and accomplishments.

Dish a little dirt by including family scandals, black sheep of the family, and skeletons in the closet. Of course, this is best done with relatives who are no longer living or for those who have given you their okay to tell it like it was.

DESIGN AND PRODUCTION: HOW TO PRODUCE CAMERA-READY ART

Desktop publishing technology made it possible for me to design and lay out a high-quality book on my home computer and laser printer. If you don't own computer equipment, check with your local library or copy shop and see if they have computers for rent. If not, you will have to hire someone to help you.

You can hire someone on staff at a quick-copy shop or a student from a local college word-processing or graphic-design training program. There are also professional trade associations in many cities. Call the trade association and ask for a referral. For example, in Chicago some trade associations are Chicago Women in Publishing, Independent Writers of Chicago, Women in Design, and the National Association of Black Journalists. Your city may have similar organizations.

There are three steps in the book production process: typesetting, editing, and design.

Typesetting

When preparing your manuscript you can do it yourself by inputting your data into a computer word-processing program or you can hire a typesetter (someone to input the data for you). Using word processing is fast and easy, and correcting errors or making changes is effortless. Word processing also allows you to spell-check the document.

Editing

Once you have your data input and your manuscript is complete, you will want to have it professionally edited. Writers cannot edit their own work; they are too close to the project and do not have an objective eye. An editor revises sentences, corrects grammar, checks for misspelled words, and performs other tasks. Again, hire a qualified college student or get a referral from a trade association. The cost is usually minimal; about one to two dollars per page, but worth every penny to eliminate mistakes and to create a professionally produced manuscript.

Design

Making your manuscript look good is the purpose of design. It is how type and pictures are combined. A book's appeal is both its editorial content and its appearance. You want to have both in your book project. You can use either word-processing or graphic page-layout software for your project.

Word Processing

When using word processing you want to decide on the style of type (called *font*) and its size (measured in points). Times and Times Roman are popular book fonts. Sizes from 10 to 12 points usually work best. Justify all your copy; that is, make all the lines even at both margins, like this type. Do not have ragged edges on the right margin. Use larger point sizes for your chapter titles.

You'll need to leave spaces on the pages where you want the pictures to go. The printer or copy shop can put them in later. Use small type (about 8 points) for captions under pictures.

For final output a laser printer is best. If you don't have one, take your disk to the library or quick-print shop and have them run off a master copy for you. Make all your subsequent copies from the master.

Page Layout Software

Page layout programs, such as Pagemaker or Quark Express, are sophisticated graphic layout software. They allow you to use many design elements. You can easily combine pictures, type, and other graphic design elements on a single page. You can also add borders and put type in two or three columns on a page. These programs are generally used by professional graphic designers who can deliver a beautifully designed book. Amateurs, however, can learn to use the programs to produce a project as well. If you are not going to utilize the page-layout software for other projects, though, it is not worth the expense or time commitment to develop a basic level of competence with the software. It makes more sense to hire a qualified freelancer at a quick-copy shop, school, or trade organization to do the work for you.

How to Print Your Manuscript

The first copies of my family book were duplicated and bound at a local quick-print shop. I made just a few copies to share with my relatives in hopes of getting donations or advance sales to do a small print run of a hundred books in time for our family reunion.

The kind of book you decide to publish depends on your financial resources: the quick-copy version was more than adequate for sharing my discoveries and it fit my budget. It won't, however, last from generation to generation the way a hardcover book will. In addition, photographs don't reproduce as well as they would in a higher-quality printed book.

The average genealogist will be producing publishing projects in quantities of fewer than five hundred. Therefore, this discussion will focus on various options for self-publishing.

Quick-Copy Shop

These shops include places like Kinko's and American Speedy Printing. Consider these shops if you're printing fewer than one hundred copies. They may no longer be cost-effective when producing more than that. Prepare camera-ready copy. This is text or art that is ready to be shot by the printer's camera. There should be no smudges or broken or unclear type in your camera-ready copy. If your camera-ready copy is complete, these shops can run off copies and provide limited kinds of book binding. The most popular methods of binding in these shops are spiral and tape. Also, there is limited choice in cover design. Usually only card stock or vinyl covers are available. These shops often have in-house designers who can help you graphically lay out and design your book.

Short–Run Printers

These printers can print your books from one hundred to one thousand copies or more. They generally use a process called off-set lithography. The quality is usually good and photo reproduction is a lot better than with quick-copy shops. You must provide these printers with camera-ready copy.

Offset printers print on large flat sheets or continuous roll paper with four, eight, sixteen, or thirty-two pages per side. Books are printed on both sides of the paper doubling these increments. Thus, the number of pages in your book should be in multiples of four. If you produce a seventy-three-page book instead of seventy-two pages, you will be charged for a seventy-six-page book even though you're only one page over.

Offset printers can also provide professionally produced traditional book covers and binding. You can select a hard or soft cover with appropriate binding. This book is an example of a softcover or paperback.

When using a traditional printer remember the 10 percent over/ under rule that often surprises self-publishers. It is difficult to stop printing presses on an exact number. Therefore, printers reserve the right to come in 10 percent over or under the target number of copies to print on a job. This is almost always specified on their estimate. It has been my experience that most printing jobs are 10 percent over. That means if your books cost $3 each to print and you print a thousand, your job should be $3,000. But with 10 percent overage, the job will actually cost $3,300 for eleven hundred books. Be sure to budget accordingly.

Docutech

The latest in short-run printing technology is the Docutech copy machine made by Xerox. Docutech is a high-speed, high-quality copy machine that can create professional-book-quality copies at speeds of over a hundred per minute. It has excellent print quality at 600 dots per inch (dpi). This is twice the quality of the average laser printer (300 dpi). Because of its high dpi, the Docutech can reproduce photos fairly well and even bind the books when finished.

I've printed two books using the Docutech machine and have been very pleased with the results. It did an excellent job with my family's photos. The quality was not as high as an offset print job might have produced, but sufficient for most genealogy projects.

You can find a Docutech machine in a few select quick-copy shops and short-run printer locations. Look up copy shops in the Yellow Pages and call around until you find a shop that has one. Then visit the shop with a few photos and pages from your publishing project and ask for a demonstration. If the quality is adequate for you then get a price estimate for your job.

If you want something of better quality, talk to a few offset printers and get estimates. Prices can vary greatly.

PRINTING CHECKLIST

The following is a checklist of things you'll need to address when printing a project.

- Estimates: Get at least three and make sure they are all in writing. Remember the 10 percent over and under rule and budget accordingly.
- Paper type: Discuss weight and quality with the printer to see how your selections will affect cost and durability.
- Cover choices: Select from card stock, hardcover, or soft-cover.
- Binding choices: Select from tape, spiral, perfect bind, saddle stitch, and so on. The type of binding you choose must correspond with the type of cover you select.
- Size of book: $5^1/2 \times 8$, 6×9, or $8^1/2 \times 11$ are the most popular sizes. The larger the book, the more paper needed and the greater the cost.
- Number of copies: How many will you print?
- Proofs: Always request a proof, often called a blueline. It is your last chance to check the document to see if everything is perfect.

How Much Will It Cost?

Wow, how much is all this going to cost? Good question. The first thing you want to do as a self-publisher is get a good understanding of the project cost, develop a budget, and determine how to raise funds. These are the key items that should be listed in your budget. Get cost estimates for each.

- Typesetting: Will you do it yourself or hire someone?
- Graphic design: Does your project need additional design or is good typesetting and layout from a word processing program adequate?
- Printing cost: Get estimates from quick-copy shops, Docutech service providers, and/or offset printers.
- Photographs: There is generally a charge for every photo because of the cost of preparing them for printing. Find out how much from the printer.

- Covers and binding: Choose the most appropriate styles and get cost estimates.
- Marketing: How will you let your relatives know about the book?

The largest expense in this list is printing. The type of printing you select and the number of books you print will determine most of your expenses. On the low end, projects average about $1,000 for fifty books (about $20 each) reproduced using a Docutech. On the high end, projects run about $4,000 (about $10 each) for four hundred hardbound books. The per-copy cost goes down as the size of your print order increases.

Where Will the Money Come From?
How to pay is for a self-publisher to figure out. Here are some suggestions.

1. Ask relatives to prepay.
2. Borrow the cost of the project from a relative. Sell the books at the family reunion and pay back the relative.
3. Ask relatives for specific donation amounts to get the books printed.
4. Advance the money for the project from your personal funds and pay yourself from book sales.

BUT I CAN'T DO THIS ALONE!
Don't panic. There are companies that specialize in helping people publish genealogy projects. They will be happy to help you through the process. There is a charge for their services. Write or call for free information. Two sources are:

Lindsey Publishing, Inc.
2023 W. Carroll Avenue, Suite F241
Chicago, IL 60612
312-226-1458

Genealogy Publishing Service
573 Beasley Mine Road
Franklin, NC 28734
704-524-7063

Additionally, a few of the current genealogy computer software programs can make a genealogy book for you. More about that in the next chapter.

Moving On

In this chapter I've talked about using computers in the production and printing process. But there is much more you can do with computer technology to enhance your genealogy research. Today, the computer can bring a wealth of genealogy information and fun to your door. The next chapter will highlight some of these opportunities.

WORKING WITH TECHNOLOGY

Genealogists must collect and organize a great deal of data. This job is made easier thanks to computers, which have become a major asset to genealogy research. Can you do genealogy without a computer? Of course you can, and many people do. These days, however, the personal computer is helping a growing number of amateur genealogists find their pasts. Hard drives, floppy disks, and software are as much the tools of a genealogist as census reports. Computers do the same things I've talked about already: prepare pedigree charts and group sheets; store data; help you research ancestors and historical information; and assist you in publishing your research findings and family history. Computers do all these tasks better and quicker than manual methods. They also give you greater flexibility for outputting data. Additionally, computer technology allows you to go online to get research by other genealogists and to use compact discs to sift through government records. You may then take what you find, enter it in genealogy software programs, and create family trees and personal files of ancestors complete with photos, video, and sound clips. This chapter will focus on these areas plus other ways technology can benefit African-American genealogists.

COMPUTER USES FOR GENEALOGY

This section is a guide to computer uses, available genealogy software, and researching on the Internet.

The Best Book

When I got my new computer I made a visit to my local library to read up on the latest methods in researching genealogy on the computer. The books were so outdated as to be no longer practical for the current age of the information superhighway. Luckily, I found an absolute gem at the bookstore. This is the best book on the subject at the time of this writing and well worth the twenty-five-dollar investment: *Your Roots: Total Genealogy Planning on Your Computer,* by Richard Eastman, Ziff Davis Publishers, 1995.

I consider this book the basic manual in getting started with computer research. It is written in clear, easy language so a beginner can understand. But what really makes it valuable is the CD-ROM packaged with it. The CD contains software demos and shareware programs you can explore before you purchase your own software, including some of those being reviewed in this chapter. It also contains a variety of forms, such as census inquiry forms and family information forms. And it provides resource information, such as the directory of the National Archives, addresses of all Vital Records offices in the United States, and a card file of over five thousand genealogy societies, libraries, and archives throughout North America. If that's not enough, it comes with fifteen dollars' worth of free time on Compuserve, a popular on-line service. The CD is for Microsoft Windows 3.1 or higher and MS-DOS 3.0 or higher base environments.

Genealogy Software

You don't have to be a computer genius to use genealogy software. You can usually learn the basics of the program by reading the quick-start section of the manual. You can generally be up and running in less than an hour. It should be no more difficult than reading the instructions for setting up your computer. Of course, you should read the entire manual when you can.

Genealogy programs let you store information on births, deaths, and marriages, and allow you to write notes for each family member. You can then view that information in several useful ways as pedigree charts, group sheets, and descendants charts. You can easily add information and make changes. Additionally, the most current information is readily available to you. The printouts are clear and ready to send to relatives for their input into your family history.

Be sure to always back up your data onto floppy disks! It is a nightmare if your disk or hard drive goes bad and all the information you painstakingly input is lost. This happened to me while I was writing my family book. The hard drive could not be repaired, and nothing could be saved since I had not backed up my data. Luckily, I had printed copies of my work.

There are many software programs from which to choose. The general rule of thumb is to purchase the best program you can afford. Make sure the software program you purchase has GEDCOM as a standard feature.

GEDCOM is a program that allows two people or institutions that store data differently to import and export data. GEDCOM is an abbreviation of **GE**nealogy **D**ata **COM**munications. The program was created by the Family History Center of the Church of Jesus Christ of Latter-Day Saints (the Mormons), and is the standard for genealogical information transfer.

Let's say you and your cousin are getting your family history together in time for the family reunion. You did part of the project in *Family Roots* software but she did her part in *Reunion* software. She can send her portion to you, and your software will be able to translate it for use in your program. GEDCOM spares you from having to rekey all this information. This is important because genealogists often send each other data using a variety of programs. Without GEDCOM you won't be able to read some of it.

Five Software Programs Reviewed

Generally, genealogy software can be purchased in both software and discount stores.

Family Roots is produced by Quinsept. It is a program that assists your search by allowing you to store a standard set of information for each family member. The program is divided into separate but integrated parts. Storage of birth, death, marriage, parents, offspring, and notes for each person is supported in one part. Another part allows you to make indexes of people in a wide variety of ways. Other parts allow you to make pedigree charts and family group sheets. *Family Roots* costs around $129; its benefits include the following:

1. The program makes good pedigree charts.
2. It is one of the few programs that come in both PC, Commodore, and Macintosh versions.
3. It is easy to input data.
4. Technical support is available.
5. The program supports GEDCOM.

Family Tree Maker is produced by Banner Blue and was the best-selling genealogy software in 1995, according to an April 1996 *Wall Street Journal* article. The company also publishes CDs containing Social Security and census records and a CD with twelve thousand family trees voluntarily submitted by its customers. *Family Tree Maker* comes in two versions, floppy disks and the deluxe CD version. The CD version includes a complete guide to getting started in genealogy and comes with 100 million names from the U.S. Census records. The program prints out great-looking charts and group sheets. This program is easy to understand and data is easy to input.

Its features are:

1. The CD version has a "how to" genealogy guide.
2. It creates great-looking printouts of charts.
3. The CD version includes 100 million names from the U.S. Census.
4. Photos can be scanned in if you have a scanner.
5. Technical support is available.
6. The program supports GEDCOM.
7. Good value: the floppy Disk costs $45, the CD: $70.
8. The program is currently available in the Windows version only.

Family Origins is produced by Parsons Technology and has a lot of kick for a great price (under $50 if purchased in discount stores). The program is easy-to-use, data entry is simple, and errors can be easily corrected. It has a huge database with room for up to thirty thousand individuals. If you have a scanner, the program fully supports scanned photographs and graphics. It can also produce a large number of printed reports like ancestor charts, family group sheets, etc. Features include the following:

1. Data entry is easy.
2. The program has photo and graphics capability.
3. The program can produce complete genealogy books of one person's descendants.
4. It can print a large number of reports.
5. It supports GEDCOM.
6. Good value: the program has a lot of features for the less than $50 price.
7. The program is available in the Windows version only.

Reunion is produced by Leister Productions. This powerful software program combines word processing, database management, and charting capabilities. Genealogy reports, such as family histories and group sheets, are easily created. It also creates mailing lists and questionnaires. You can create color graphic charts, if you have a color printer, and if you have a scanner, you can scan in photographs. *Reunion* is a very high-end, state-of-the-art program but it's also pricey at $160. Features include the following:

1. Powerful, beautifully combining database capabilities, graphics, and text.
2. It uses your existing word processor to create charts and reports.
3. You can scan in photos.
4. It comes in Windows and Macintosh versions.
5. Technical support is available.
6. The program supports GEDCOM.
7. Pricey at $160.

Roots IV is the latest version of genealogy software produced by Commsoft, Inc., a company with longevity in this business. Like *Reunion,* this is a high-end program with great features. The strongest is its printed reports. From these reports the program can help you create your genealogy book. Of course, it does an excellent job in handling any data you input, and photographs can be scanned into the program. The program works with most printers but you'll need a laser printer to benefit from its graphics capability. It takes a while to get the hang of this program, but the manual is well written but a hefty five hundred pages long. Features include:

1. It is a powerful high-end program.
2. It produces a wide variety of reports that can help create a genealogy book.
3. The graphics capabilities are very sophisticated, but a laser printer is required to take advantage of them. However, the program works well with dot-matrix and ink-jet printers.
4. Photos can be scanned in.

5. Technical support is available.
6. The program supports GEDCOM.
7. It offers a good value at a mid-price of $125.
8. It is a challenging program recommended for those who are computer savvy and have the time to learn the program's features.
9. It supports MS-DOS and Windows 3.1, but a Windows 95 version is in the works.

Word Processing

A word processor can also be used to record genealogy information and to create documents. The advantage of genealogy software is that if you make a change in one database, it's immediately changed in the program's other databases. With word processing, you'd have to go through and make each change manually.

Word processing is getting so sophisticated now, even images can be input into documents. Plus, newsletters to keep your family updated on your findings can now be done using word processing. It's perfect for writing a letter requesting information from relatives. You can write one letter and mail merge the addresses from your database so each relative gets a personal letter even though you only typed it once.

Word processing is also useful for creating an autobiographical sketch of an ancestor or a report on your research findings. Many libraries have computers you can use free of charge, all with word processing capabilities.

RESEARCH USES

The computer is more than just a place to store your data and publish your work. It is also a wonderful tool for doing research. Unless you just moved here from another planet, you have surely heard about the information superhighway and the World

Wide Web. Originally I had doubts about whether computer research could benefit African-American genealogist, but I was wrong. Genealogy research on the Internet is a wonderful resource.

Even if you don't have a computer you can still use this technology. You can always rent Internet time at the local library, some bookstores, or one of the Internet coffee shops that are springing up around the country.

Although this is not a book on computer training, I do want to suggest some ways to use the computer to research your African-American genealogy. First let's get clear about the difference between on-line services, the World Wide Web, and the Internet. Second, there are a few other terms we need to define.

On-line services are private information providers such as America Online, Compuserve, and Prodigy. They are an excellent way for a beginner to start because they have organized a lot of data for you that is available with a click of your mouse or keyboard. They charge a monthly fee, usually from $8 to $10, for about five hours of usage per month. There is an additional charge for more hours. On-line services provide easy internet access for subscribers.

There are also independent internet access providers that provide unlimited access for a monthly fee of $19.95. These don't have the bells and whistles of on-line services, but they're efficient, effective, and cheaper. AT&T has such a service but there are many more. Check your local yellow pages.

The Internet is a vast network of computers that allows businesses, schools, government agencies, and individuals to exchange information on any subject. You can chat with people around the world, download information from various files, research information, and exchange e-mail.

The World Wide Web is the multimedia segment of the Internet allowing for the use of text, graphics, and sound. Web sites consist of electronic pages that are connected to one another within the same site or through other sites. You can

8. MISSISSIPPI STATE UNIVERSITY—AFRICAN AMERICAN HISTORY SITE This is a good source for information on the Museum of the History of Slavery of the Atlantic, Underground Railroad, Canadian black history, black history pioneers, buffalo soldiers, events and people in black history, and more.

URL: http://www.msstate.edu/Archives/History/USA/Afro-Amer/afro.html

9. BUFFALO SOLDIERS This site provides information on the U.S. Army 9th and 10th Calvary formed after the Civil War.

URL: http://www.horseworld.com/lmh/buf/buftoc.html

10. AFRICAN-AMERICAN PUBLICATIONS This site provides information on black newspapers and has great links to numerous African-American sites on the Internet.

URL: http://www.bnl.com/aasm/pubs.html

11. NEW ORLEANS LIBRARY The Louisiana division of this library has extensive African-American genealogy resources. This is an excellent web site for anyone researching his or her ancestry in New Orleans. It contains a detailed listing of its holdings, including an obituary index, 1804–1972, census records, and marriage records. It also has Family Search, an automated, CD-ROM–based resource offering a wide variety of genealogical information from such sources as the Social Security Death Index, the LDS International Genealogical Index, and the LDS Ancestral file.

URL: http://www.gnofn.org/whs1/government/local/black.html

12. AFRICAN-AMERICAN ARCHAEOLOGY HOME PAGE Review this page to get information on New York's African-American burial ground project.

URL: http://www.mindspring.com/~wheaton/Winter1994.html

13. CLP PENNSYLVANIA DEPT-RESOURCES IN AFRICAN-AMERICAN GENEALOGY This web site contains a detailed listing of the items contained in their collection, which includes books, handbooks, locality guides, slave census indexes, etc.

URL: http://www.clpgh.org/CLP/Pennsylvania/oak_penna32.html

14. CHICAGO: DESTINATION FOR THE GREAT MIGRATION This web site provides information on the great migration of African-Americans from the South to Northern cities, focusing on Chicago. It includes a map of ethnic neighborhoods, and a discussion of the *Chicago Defender* newspaper's successful campaign to urge blacks to migrate to Chicago as well as the realities faced when they arrived in the "promised land."

URL: http://www.loc.gov/exhibits/African/chi.html

15. AFRICAN-AMERICAN MOSAIC This web site includes highlights of the Library of Congress Resource Guide for the Study of Black History and Culture. It is the first library-wide resource guide to the institution's African-American collection.

URL: http://www.loc.gov/exhibits/African/intro.html

16. AFRICAN-AMERICAN WEB CONNECTION and **UNIVERSAL BLACK PAGES** These are web-site directories that provide information for people looking for Internet sources related to topics of interest to African-Americans, both contemporary and historic.

URL: http://www.aawc.com/aawc.com/aawc.html

URL: http://www.gatech.edu/bgsa/blackpages/business.html

17. BLACK LANDS: INTERNET DIRECTORY Another web site providing information on history, historical figures, genealogy mailing lists, etc., of interest to African-American researchers.

URL: http://www.pinki.com/BL/history.html

18. KENTUCKY DEPARTMENT FOR LIBRARIES AND ARCHIVES This web site is a description of their genealogical holdings. The

African-American genealogical sources available for research include Kentucky slave censuses, birth and death records, county deed books, and manumission reports. If researching in this state, be sure to review the List of Dower Slaves. Many slaveholders were required to submit an annual list to the county clerk of the names, sex, and ages of their slaves. A rare find indeed.

URL: http//www.kdla.state.ky.us

19. A STUDENT'S GUIDE TO AFRICAN-AMERICAN GENEALOGY
This is the home page for this book by Anne E. Johnson and published by Oryx Press. The book is a guide to help young people begin to trace their genealogy.

URL: http://www.oryxpress.com/authors/a00230.html

20. U.S. NATIONAL ARCHIVES AND RECORDS ADMINISTRATION AND U.S. BUREAU OF THE CENSUS Both of these have home pages you can access. Information is limited but includes locations and operating times.

URL: http://www.nara.gov

URL: http://www.census.gov

WHAT KINDS OF RESULTS CAN YOU EXPECT?

Two months after I posted my family name in the genealogy posting section, I got an e-mail from a man who had been researching the Parker family from Harris County, Georgia. I e-mailed him back and briefly told him my family lineage. He turned out to be a cousin and a resource gold mine. My great-grandfather and his great-grandmother were brother and sister. I asked him for any Parker photographs he might have, since the family book I'd written has lots of pictures of Gores but not many of Parkers. Incredibly, he had pictures of the Parkers, including one of my great-grandfather Julius, his great-grandmother Martha and her child, and one of Julius's brother Isaiah and his entire family. He made copies and sent them to me. He also knew of other Parker family members who were researching our lineage and sent me their e-mail addresses, telephone numbers, and mailing addresses. One of these cousins, Lorraine Hargray-Reid, had also written a story called *My Grandmother's Story.* The whole experience was like having a family reunion via the Internet.

The Internet can also be a good site for researching historical background information. For example, the Civil War has its own special interest groups on America Online. The fifty-thousand-plus sources for African-American genealogy posted by Webcrawler included volumes of sources on African-American history.

Computer software programs can help you organize and save your data. Additionally, through the use of on-line services and Internet access providers, you can do research that might not be available in your local library or National Archive research center. You can literally connect to thousands of computers for information on African-American genealogy and history. Of course, like every other aspect of genealogy research, you never know what you're going to find until you start digging.

Technology is an asset in the compiling, storing, and retrieving of information. It is also a valuable asset in publishing your findings, as discussed in Chapter 6.

It is also a great communication tool. If you'd like to write me about how your genealogy research is progressing, just send me an e-mail at: DBeas22685@aol.com.

Appendixes

AFRICAN-AMERICAN HISTORICAL AND GENEALOGICAL SOCIETIES

Many different types of organizations are listed here. The National Afro-American Historical and Genealogical Society (AAHGS), headquartered in Washington, D.C., has many affiliates and chapters throughout the United States. These AAHGS affiliates are so noted.

AAHGS— U.S. National Headquarters

Afro-American Historical and
  Genealogical Society, Inc.
1700 Shepherd Street NW
Washington, D.C. 20011

Arizona

AAHGS—Tucson
P.O. Box 58272
Tucson, AZ 87554

Buffalo Soldiers Historical
Society, Inc.
324 West Aspen
P.O. Box 937
Flagstaff, AZ 86001

California

Afro-American Genealogical Society
600 State Drive
Exposition Park
Los Angeles, CA 90037

Black Military History Society
1793 Geary Street
San Francisco, CA 94115

Canada

Black Cultural Centre for Nova Scotia
P.O. Box 2128 East Dartmouth
Nova Scotia B2W 3Y2 Canada

Colorado

The Black Genealogy Search Group
P.O. Box 40674
Denver, CO 80204-0674

Florida

AAHGS—Central Florida
P.O. Box 5742
Deltona, FL 32728

Georgia

African-American Family History
 Association
C2077 Bent Creek Way SW
Atlanta, GA 30311

Illinois

AAHGS—Little Egypt
703 South Wall Street, #5
Carbondale, IL 62901

AAHGS—Patricia Liddell Researchers
P.O. Box 438652
Chicago, IL 60643

Afro-American Genealogical and
 Historical Society of Chicago
P.O. Box 37-7651
Chicago, IL 60637

Indiana

Indiana African-American Historical
 and Genealogical Society
502 Clover Terrace
Bloomington, IN 47404-1809

Louisiana

Afro-Louisiana Historical and
 Genealogical Society
P.O. Box 2247
Baton Rouge, LA 70821

Maryland

AAHGS—Central Maryland
P.O. Box 2774
Columbia, MD 21045

AAHGS—Prince Georges
County
P.O. Box 447772
Fort Washington, MD 20744-9998

Michigan

Fred Hart Williams Genealogical
 Society
Burton Historical Collection
5201 Woodward Avenue
Detroit, MI 48202

Missouri

AAHGS—Landon Cheek
P.O. Box 23804
St. Louis, MO 63121-0840

AAHGS—MAGIC
3700 Blue Parkway
Kansas City, MO 64130

New Jersey

AAHGS—New Jersey
785 Sterling Drive East
South Orange, NJ 07079

New York

AAHGS—JSS Greater New York
P.O. Box 022340
Brooklyn, NY 11201

North Carolina

Afro-American Family History Project
P.O. Box 6074
Greensboro, NC 27405

North Carolina Afro-American
 Heritage Society
P.O. 26334
Raleigh, NC 27611

Ohio

African-American Genealogical
 Society of Cleveland
P.O. Box 200382
Cleveland, OH 44120

Pennsylvania

AAHGS—Western Pennsylvania
P-1832 Runnette Street
Pittsburgh, PA 15235

African-American Genealogy Group
P.O. Box 1798
Philadelphia, PA 19105

Rhode Island

Rhode Island Black Heritage Society
46 Aborn Street
Providence, RI 02903

Tennessee

African-American Genealogical
 and Historical Society
P.O. Box 17684
Nashville, TN 37217

Texas

AAHGS—Houston
P.O. Box 750877
Houston, TX 77275-0877

Tarrant County Black History and
 Genealogical Society
1020 East Humboldt
Fort Worth, TX 76104

Virginia

AAHGS—Hampton Roads
P.O. Box 2448
Newport News, VA 23609

AAHGS—Tidewater Chapter
2200 Crossroad Trail
Virginia Beach, VA 23456

Washington, D.C.

AAHGS, D.C.—James Dent Walker
P.O. Box 34683
Washington, D.C. 20043

LIBRARIES AND CONSULATES

National Archives—Regional Archive Facilities

National Archives-New England Region
380 Trapelo Road
Waltham, MA 02154-6399
Phone: 617-647-8100
Fax: 617-647-8460
Internet: archives@waltham.nara.gov
Hours: 8:00 AM–4:30 PM, Monday–Friday; 8:00 AM–4:30 PM, 1st Saturday of each month
Serves Connecticut, Maine, Massachusetts, New Hampshire, Rhode Island, and Vermont.

National Archives-Pittsfield Region
100 Dan Fox Drive
Pittsfield, MA 01201-8230
Phone: 413-445-6885
Fax: 413-445-7599
Internet: archives@pittsfield.nara.gov
Hours: 9:00 AM–3:00 PM, Monday–Friday; 9:00 AM–9:00 PM, Wednesday
Microfilm only.

National Archives-Northeast Region
201 Varick Street
New York, NY 10014-4811
Phone: 212-337-1300
Fax: 212-337-1306
Internet: archives@newyork.nara.gov
Hours: 8:00 AM–4:30 PM, Monday–Friday; 8:30 AM–4:00 PM, 3rd Saturday of
each month
Serves New Jersey, New York, Puerto Rico, and the U.S. Virgin Islands.

National Archives-Mid Atlantic Region
900 Market Street, Room 1350
Philadelphia, PA 19107-4292
Phone: 215-597-3000
Fax: 215-597-2303
Internet: archives@philarch.nara.gov
Hours: 8:00 AM–5:00 PM, Monday–Friday; 8:00 AM–4:00 PM, 2nd Saturday of
each month
Serves Delaware, Maryland, Pennsylvania, Virginia, and
West Virginia.

National Archives-Southeast Region
1557 St. Joseph Avenue
East Point, GA 30344-2593
Phone: 404-763-7477
Fax: 404-763-7033
Internet: archives@atlanta.nara.gov
Hours: 8:00 AM–4:00 PM, Monday, Wednesday, Thursday, Friday;
8:00 AM–8:00 PM, Tuesday
Serves Alabama, Florida, Georgia, Kentucky, Mississippi, North Carolina,
South Carolina, and Tennessee.

National Archives-Great Lakes Region
7358 South Pulaski Road
Chicago, IL 60629-5898
Phone: 312-353-0162
Fax: 312-353-1294
Internet: archvies@chicago.nara.gov
Hours: 8:00 AM–4:15 PM, Monday, Wednesday, Thursday, Friday;
8:00 AM–8:30 PM, Tuesday
Serves Illinois, Indiana, Michigan, Minnesota, Ohio, and Wisconsin.

National Archives-Central Plains Region
2312 East Bannister Road
Kansas City, Missouri 64131
Phone: 816-926-6272
Fax: 816-926-6982
Internet: archives@kansascity.nara.gov
Hours: 8:00 AM–4:00 PM, Monday–Friday; 9:00 AM–4:00 PM, 3rd Saturday of each month
Serves Iowa, Kansas, Missouri, and Nebraska.

National Archives-Southwest Region
501 West Felix Street, Building 1
P.O. Box 6216
Fort Worth, TX 76115-3405
Phone: 817-334-5525
Fax: 817-334-5621
Internet: archives@ftworth.nara.gov
Hours: 8:00 AM–4:00 PM, Monday–Friday
Serves Arkansas, Louisiana, Oklahoma, and Texas.

National Archives-Rocky Mountain Region
Denver Federal Center, Building 48
P.O. Box 25307
Denver, CO 80225-0307
Phone: 303-326-0817
Fax: 303-236-9354
Internet: archives@denver.nara.gov
Hours: 7:30 AM–4:00 PM, Monday, Tuesday, Thursday, Friday;
7:30 AM–5:00 PM, Wednesday
Serves Colorado, Montana, New Mexico, North Dakota, South Dakota, Utah, and Wyoming.

National Archives-Pacific Southwest Region
24000 Avila Road, 1st Floor East
P.O. Box 6719
Laguna Niguel, CA 92607-6719
Phone: 714-360-2641
Fax: 714-360-2644
Internet: archives@laguna.nara.gov
Hours: 8:00 AM–4:30 PM, Monday–Friday; 8:00 AM–4:30 PM, 1st Saturday each month (Microfilm research only)

Arizona, Southern California, and Clark County, Nevada
National Archives-Pacific Sierra Region
1000 Commodore Drive
San Bruno, CA 94066-2350
Phone: 415-876-9009
Fax: 415-876-9233
Internet: archives@sanbruno.nara.gov
Hours: 8:00 AM–4:00 PM, Monday, Tuesday, Thursday, Friday;
8:00 AM–8:00 PM, Wednesday
Serves Northern California, Hawaii, Nevada except Clark County,
the Pacific Trust Territories, and American Samoa.

National Archives-Pacific Northwest Region
6125 Sand Point Way NE
Seattle, WA 98115-7433
Phone: 206-526-6507
Fax: 206-526-4344
Internet: archives@seattle.nara.gov
Hours: 7:45 AM–4:00 PM, Monday–Friday; 5:00 PM–9:00 PM,
1st Tuesday of each month
Serves Idaho, Oregon, and Washington.

National Archives-Alaska Region
654 West Third Avenue
Anchorage, AL 99501-2145
Phone: 907-271-2441
Fax: 907-271-2442
Internet: archives@alaska.nara.gov
Hours: 8:00 AM–4:00 PM Monday–Friday; call for Saturday hours
Serves Alaska.

LIBRARIES WITH GENEALOGICAL COLLECTIONS

The Allen County Public Library
Public Library of Fort Wayne
301 West Wayne Street
Fort Wayne, IN 46802
(Begin with the index to African-American genealogy sources.)

American Genealogical Lending Library
P.O. Box 244
Bountiful, UT 84011

Burton Collection
Detroit Public Library
5201 Woodward Avenue
Detroit, MI 48202
(Begin with the index to African-American genealogy sources.)

Confederate Research Center at Hill College
P.O. Box 619
Hillsboro, TX 76645

Everton Publisher's Library
3223 South Main
Nibley, UT 84321

Genealogical Center Library
P.O. Box 71343
Marietta, GA 30007-1343

Family History Library of the Church of Jesus Christ
of Latter-Day Saints
35 North West Temple
Salt Lake City, UT 84150

Library of Congress
Local History and Genealogy Division
Washington, D.C. 20540

Los Angeles Public Library
630 West Fifth Street
Los Angeles, CA 90071
(Begin with the index to African-American genealogy sources.)

National Archives
Eighth Street and Pennsylvania Avenue NW
Washington, D.C. 20408

National Society Daughters of the American
Revolution Library
1776 D Street NW
Washington, D.C. 20006-5303

Newberry Library
60 West Walton
Chicago, IL 60610
(Begin with the index to African-American genealogy sources.)

New England Historic Genealogical Society (NEHGS)
101 Newbury Street
Boston, MA 02116
(This is the oldest genealogical organization in the world.)

New York Public Library
Fifth Avenue and Forty-second Street
New York, NY 10022

Philadelphia Public Library
Home of the Pennsylvania Abolition Society and
the Genealogy Society of Pennsylvania
1901 Bine Street
Philadelphia, PA 19103

Schomburg Center for Research in Black Culture
The New York Public Library
515 Malcolm X Boulevard
New York, NY 10027

Stagecoach Library for Genealogical Research
1840 South Wolcott Court
Denver, CO 80219

State Historical Society of Wisconsin
816 State Street
Madison, WI 53703

Robert W. Woodruff Library
Black Culture Collection
Atlanta University Center
111 James P. Brawley Drive SW
Atlanta, GA 30314
(Begin with the Slaughter Collection with over 6,000 titles.)

Vivian G. Harsh Research Collection of African-American History and Literature
Woodson Regional Library of the Chicago Public Library
9501 South Halsted
Chicago, IL 60628

AFRICAN EMBASSIES IN THE UNITED STATES

Embassy of Gambia
1030 Fifteenth Street NW
Suite 720
Washington, D.C. 20005

Embassy of Ghana
2460 Sixteenth Street NW
Washington, D.C. 20009

Embassy of Guinea
2112 Leroy Place NW
Washington, D.C. 20008

Embassy of Guinea-Bissau
211 East Forty-third Street, Suite 604
New York, NY 10017

Embassy of Liberia
5201 Sixteenth Street NW
Washington, D.C. 20011

Embassy of Senegal
2112 Wyoming Avenue NW
Washington, D.C. 20008

U.S. EMBASSIES IN WEST AFRICA
Gambia
Kairaba Avenue
P.M.B. No. 19
Banjul, Gambia

Ghana
Ring Road East
P.O. Box 194
Accra, Ghana

Guinea

B.P. 603
Conakry, Guinea

Guinea-Bissau

Avenida Domingos Ramos
CP 297
Bissau, Guinea-Bissau

Liberia

111 United Nations Drive
P.O. Box 98
Mamba Point, Monrovia

Senegal

Avenue Jean XXIII
B.P. 49
Dakar, Senegal

Sierra Leone

Corner Walpole and Siaka Stevens Street
Freetown, Sierra Leone

ADDITIONAL AFRICAN RESOURCES

Gambia

Gambia National Archives
Banjul, Gambia

Gambia National Library
Independence Drive
P.O. Box 552
Banjul, Gambia

Ghana

Ghana National Museum
Barnes Road
P.O. Box 3343
Accra, Ghana

National Archives of Ghana
P.O. Box 3056
Accra, Ghana

Research Library of African Affairs
P.O. Box 2970
Accura, Ghana

West African Historical Museum
P.O. Box 502
Cape Coast, Ghana

Guinea

Archives Nationales
B.P. 561 Bis
Conakry, Guinea

Bibliothèque Nationale
B.P. 561
Conakry, Guinea

Liberia

Africana Museum
Cuttington University College
P.O. Box 277
Monrovia, Liberia

National Museum
Monrovia, Liberia

Senegal
Archives de Senegal
Avenue Roume
Dakar, Senegal

Musée Historique
Gorée, Senegal

Sierra Leone
Public Archives of Sierra Leone
c/o Fourah Bay College Library
P.O. Box 87
Freetown, Sierra Leone

STATE RESOURCES

This partial listing of state resources is compiled from the following sources: (1) African-American family history and bibliography listings from the Newberry Library in Chicago; (2) Vivian G. Harsh Research Collection at the Woodson Regional Library in Chicago; and the Allen County Public Library in Fort Wayne, Indiana. This information can also often be found in state archives and some local libraries.

Alabama

Mills, Gary B. "Free African-Americans in Pre-Civil War 'Anglo' Alabama: Slave Manumissions Gleaned from County Court Records." *National Genealogical Society Quarterly* 83, no. 2 (June 1995).

Pinkard, Ophelia Taylor. *Descendants of Shandy Wesley Jones and Evalina Love Jones: The Story of an African-American Family of Tuscaloosa, Alabama.* Baltimore: Gateway, 1993.

Arkansas

Bureau of Refugees, Freedmen, and Abandoned Lands. Arkansas Field Office Records. Microfilm number 1171.

Although not keyed specifically to this microfilm set, the researcher should consult Volume 1 of the *Preliminary Inventory of the Records of the Field Offices of the Bureau of Refugees, Freedmen, and Abandoned Lands* (call no.: oE185.2.U56) for an inventory of the records reproduced on this microfilm.

The Newberry Library's computer catalog lists the field office towns represented on each reel. Genealogical highlights of these records include: Marriages for the period of approximately 1865–68 in field office records for Arkadelphia (reel 1), Jacksonport (reel 7), Little Rock (reels 11–13), Osceola (reel 1), Paraclifta (reel 16), Pine Bluff (reels 16–17), and Washington (reels 20–21); and labor contracts in field office records for Arkadelphia (reel 1), Augusta (reel 1), Camden (reel 2), Devall's Bluff (reel 3), Fort Smith (reels 4–5), Hamhurg (reels 5–?), Jacksonport (reel 7), Lake Village and Luna Landing (reels 7–8), Madison (reels 13–14), Monticello (reel 15), Napoleon (reel 15), Osceola (reel 16), Paraclifta (reel 16), Princeton (reel 20), and Washington (reel 21). These listings are provided to alert the researcher to the records with the greatest genealogical potential; however, these suggestions should not be relied on exclusively. The serious researcher is urged to consult the *Preliminary Inventory* in conjunction with the Newberry Library's computer catalog entry for the field office records.

Records of the Arkansas Claims Division, Disbursing Officers Claims Agents. Microfilm Number 1170. These records are primarily claims of U.S. Colored Troops soldiers for bounty and back pay. The most informative are the claims of widows or other family members relating to deceased veterans, although these are very much in the minority. Organization is chronological for letters and papers sent and received. There is periodic indexing by ledger, but even so, a scan of these records (on six reels) will take some time.

Connecticut

Brown, Barbara W., and James M. Rose. *Black Roots in Southeastern Connecticut 1650–1900*. Detroit: Gale, 1980.

District of Columbia

Haizlip, Shirlee Taylor. *The Sweeter the Juice*. New York: Simon and Schuster, 1994. An account of racial identification and family history. One branch of the family "passed" as white, while the other did not.

Sluby, P. E. Newspaper Obituary Clippings from the "Baltimore Afro-American" and the "Washington Afro-American" for the Year 1991 (call no.: foF189.B19N46).

Florida

"The Archives of the Spanish Government of West Florida (1782–1816) and African-American Research." *Journal of the AAHGS* 14-3/4 (1995).

Fears, Mary L. Jackson. *Slave Ancestral Research: It's Something Else*. Bowie, Md.: Heritage Books, 1995. This is a detailed case study narrative involving the records of Taylor, Talbot, Baldwin, and Warren counties. Surnames include McCants, McCrary, and Riley. Also see the *Supplement to the Jackson-Moore Family History and Genealogy*.

Jupiter, Del Alexa Eagan. *Augustina of Spanish West Florida and Her Descendants with Related Families of Eagan, Relker, Palmer, and Taylor*. Franklin, N.C.: Genealogy Publishing Service, 1994.

Warner, Lee H. *Freemen in an Age of Servitude: Three Generations of a Black Family*. (Proctor family). Lexington, Ky.: University Press of Kentucky, 1992.

Wells, Sharon. *Forgotten Legacy: Blacks in Nineteenth Century Key West.* Key West, Fla.: Historic Key West Preservation Board, 1982.

Georgia

Lunceford, Alvin Mell, Jr. *Taliaferro County, Georgia Records and Notes.* Spartanburg, S.C.: Reprint Company, 1988. Especially noteworthy for African-American genealogy with the inclusion of black marriage registers, the free black registry, and records by name of slaves in will and deed abstracts.

Ray, David Thornton, ed. *Black Marriage Records, Harris County, Georgia: Vol. I 1866–1923.* Hartwell, Ga.: Savannah River Valley Genealogical Society, 1994.

Stewart, Roma Jones. *Africans in Georgia, 1870.* Chicago: Homeland Publications, 1993.

Turner, Freda Reed. *Henry County, Georgia 1821–1894: Marriages, Colored/Freedmen; Record of Sales; Inventory; and Wills.* Roswell, Ga.: Wolfe Publishing, 1995.

Illinois

Brasfield, Curtis G. *The Ancestry of Mayor Harold Washington (1922–1987).* Bowie, Md.: Heritage Books, 1993.

History of Altgeld Gardens, 1944–1960. Chicago: Altgeld Carver Alumni Association, 1993.

Sapp, Peggy Lathrop. *Madison County Court Records (1˜13 1818) and Indenture Records 1805–1˜2˜, Register of Slaves, Indentured Servants, and Free Persons of Color.* Springfield, Ill.: Folkworks, 1993.

Stephens, Edythe. *African Americans of Edgar County. Illinois.* (call no.: foF547.E25A47 19gO).

Indiana

Indiana Negro Registers. Bowie, Md.: Heritage Books, 1994. Includes registers from Bartholomew, Floyd, Franklin, Gibson, Harrison, Hendricks, Jackson, Jefferson, Jennings, Knox, Martin, Ohio, Orange, Switzerland, and Washington counties.

Robbins, Coy D. *Forgotten Hoosiers: African Heritage in Orange County.* Bowie. Md.: Heritage Books, 1994.

Kentucky

"Declaration of Marriage of Negroes and Mulattos, Nelson County, Kentucky, 1866–1872." *Kentucky Ancestors* 30, no. 3 (1995): call no.: OF450.K4

"Deed of Emancipation of James Norris." *Mississippi River Routes* 1, no. 2 (Winter 1993). Norris was a Bracken County indentured servant identified in Warren County, Mississippi.

Schmitzer, Jeanne Cannella. "Index to the 'Registers of Signatures of Depositors in the Freedmen's Savings and Trust Company 1865–1874,' Lexington, Kentucky, Branch: March 21, 1870–July 3, 1874." *Kentucky Ancestors* 29, no. 4 (1993–1994) and 30, no. 1 (1994–1995). See also the *Journal of the AAHGS* 14, no. 1 & 2 (1995).

Sprague, Stuart Seely. "Freedmen's Bureau Marriage Records of Warren, Montgomery, and Clark counties, Kentucky, in the National Archives." *Kentucky Ancestors* 30, no. 2 (1994–1995). This article was adapted from the Freedmen's Bureau field office records, National Archives RG 105.

Louisiana

Brasseaux, Carl A. *Creoles of Color in the Bayou Country.* Jackson, Miss.: University Press of Mississippi, 1994.

Freedmen's Savings and Trust Signature Books. Microfilm call number 709. Records for New Orleans and Shreveport on reel 12.

Maryland

Arpee, Marion. "Maryland Slaves in Hardey Wills and Indentures: 1718–1805." *Maryland Genealogical Society Bulletin* 22, no. 1 (Winter 1981). Applicable for Prince George's and Charles counties.

Behrend, Carolyn. "Charles Carroll of Carrolltown Inventory of Property Slave List." *Maryland Genealogical Society Bulletin* 23, no. 4 (Fall 1982).

Callum, Agnes Kane. "Progenitors of a Black Family: Raphael and Hillery Cane 1793–1890." *Maryland Genealogical Society Bulletin* 21, no. 2 (Spring 1980).

Clayton, Ralph. *Slavery, Slaveholding, and the Free Black Population of Antebellum Baltimore.* Bowie, Md.: Heritage Books, 1993 Contains extensive source material including listings of applications for certificates of freedom; Maryland Colonization Society gleanings from the *Baltimore Sun;* free blacks in the 1831 Baltimore city directory; free blacks and slaves in the 1850 census; mortality schedules; and abstracts from the general population census schedules for various years.

Potter, Alice E. "Slaves in Joseph Taylor's Will." *Maryland Genealogical Society Bulletin* 22, no. 3 (Summer 1981). Applicable to Baltimore County, 1789.

"Raphael Cane and his Descendants." *Maryland Genealogical Society Bulletin* 21, no. 3 (Summer 1980).

Sluby, P. E. *Newspaper Obituary Clippings from the "Baltimore Afro-American" and the "Washington Afro-American" for the Year 1991* (call no.: foF189.B19N46).

Stuart, Karen. "Early Vital Records of Blacks in All Hallows Parish, Anne Arundel County." *Maryland Genealogical Society Bulletin* 31, no. 2 (Spring 1990).

Michigan

Claspy, Everett. *The Negro in Southwestern Michigan: Negroes in the North in a Rural Environment.* Dowagiac, Mich.: Claspy, 1967.

Cox, Anna-Lisa. "A Pocket of Freedom: Blacks in Covert, Michigan in the Nineteenth Century." *Michigan Historical Review* 21, no. 1 (Spring 1995).

Mississippi

Archer, Chalmers. *Growing Up Black in Rural Mississippi: Memories of Family, Heritage of a Place.* New York: Walker, 1992. History of the Archer family in Holmes County.

"Deed of Emancipation of James Norris." *Mississippi River Routes* 1, no. 2 (Winter 1993). Norris was a Bracken County, Kentucky, indentured servant certified in Warren County in 1819.

Dimond, E. Grey, and Herman Hattaway, eds. *Letters from Forest Place: A Plantation Family's Correspondence 1846–1881.* Jackson, Miss.: University Press of Mississippi, 1993. The Watkins plantation in Carroll County included approximately seventy-five slaves, some of whom are mentioned in the correspondence.

"Early Jefferson County African Americans." *Mississippi River Routes* 1, no. 3 (Spring 1994).

"Freedmen's Marriage Records, Issaquena County, M~." *Mississippi River Routes* 1, no. 1 (Fall 1993).

Haymon, Serena Abbess. *Amite County, Mississippi 1920 School Census (Black).* Greenwood Springs, La.: Haymon, 1990.

———. *Amite County, Mississippi 1920–23 School Census (Black).* Greenwood Springs, La.: Haymon, 1990.

———. *Amite County, Mississippi 1924 School Census (Black).* Baton Rouge, La.: F and M Enterprises, 1993.

———. *Amite County, Mississippi 1927 School Census (Black).* Baton Rouge, La.: F and M Enterprises, 1989.

————. *Amite County, Mississippi Cemeteries (African American)*. Baton Rouge, La.: F and M Enterprises, 1993.

Mississippi Department of Archives and History. *Mississippi Freedmen's Bureau Labor Contracts Index*. Microfiche number 2588. Indexes to reel and microfilm *counter* number. (This is applicable only to a few microfilm readers.)

"Nancy Watts' Will: A Free Woman of Colour." *Mississippi River Routes* 1, no. 1 (Fall 1993). Watts was a Claiborne County resident.

Terry, Brenda. *Slaves I. Claiborne County, Mississippi*. Bowie, Md.: Heritage Books, 1995.

Missouri

Blattner, Teresa. *People of Color: Black Genealogical Records and Abstracts from Missouri Sources*. Bowie, Md.: Heritage Books, 1993. This is a multivolume set.

Roulhac, Roy L. "Civil War Military and Pension Records: The Roulhacs." *Journal of the AAHGS* 14, nos. 3/4 (1995).

North Carolina

Rowe, Carolyn Corpening. "Index of Catawba County, North Carolina African-American Marriages, 1867–1907." *Journal of the AAHGS* 14, nos. 1/2 (1995).

"Sales of Slaves in Burke County, North Carolina, 1791–1851." *Journal of the AAHGS* 13, nos. 1/2 (Spring/Fall 1994).

Taylor, Margaret Smith. "Smith/Buckland Cemetery and Robert Smith Cemetery, Gates County, North Carolina." *Journal of the AAHGS* 14, nos. 1/2 (1995).

White, Barnetta McGhee. *Enslaved Ancestors Abstracted from Deed Books: Granville County, North Carolina*. Durham, N.C.: 1993.

Williams, Margo Lee. "The Division of Lands of Miles Lassiter." *Journal of the AAHGS* 14, nos. 1 & 2 (1995): Applicable to Randolph County.

Willis, Eulis A. *Navassa: The Town and Its People 1735–1991.* Navassa, N.C.: Eulis A. Willis, 1993.

Wynne, Frances Holloway. *North Carolina Extant Voter Registrations of 1867.* Bowie, Md.: Heritage Books, 1992. Although the voter registration records for many counties have not survived, these records can be especially significant for African-American genealogical research, given their midway point between emancipation and the 1870 census.

Ohio

Clay, Sheila J. Farmer. *The Stillgess-Chavers Family Genealogy.* Dayton, Ohio: Sheila J. Farmer Clay, 1994. Other families, most with Champaign County connections, are Farmer, Roberts, and Duncan.

Sacks, Howard L. *Way Up North in Dixie: A Black Family's Claim to the Confederate Anthem.* Washington, D.C.: Smithsonian Institute, 1993. History of the Snowden family.

Williams, Jacob C. Lillie: Black Life in Martins Ferry, Ohio during the 1920s and 1930s. Ann Arbor, Mich.: 1991.

Oklahoma (Indian Territory)

Enrollment Cards for the Five Civilized Tribes, 1898–1914. Microfilm number 1083. The Newberry Library's holdings are incomplete at this writing; however, the following reels are available and may be of interest to African-American researchers: Index (reel 1); Cherokee freedmen enrollments 1–1595 (reels 23–26); Cherokee freedmen minor enrollments 1–542 (reels 26–27); and Cherokee freedmen D1 D1342, R1-R1276 (reels 33–38). Consult the Index reel first.

Page, Jo Ann Curtis. *Descendants of Joseph Lynch and Sophie Ross.* Chicago: Jo Ann Curtis Page, 1994.

———. *Descendants of Samuel and Maria Riley.* Chicago: Jo Ann Curtis Page, 1994.

Pennsylvania

Harris, Richard E. Politics and Prejudice: A History of Chester (Pa.) Negroes. Apache Junction, Ariz.: Relmo, 1991.

South Carolina

Matthews, Harry Bradshaw. *Killingsworth and Isaac the African: An Intercultural Saga.* Gettysburg, Pa.: Gettysburg College and the Intercultural Resource Center, 1987.

Prince George Winyah Church (Charleston) Register. Microfiche number 608. Microfiche of baptismal and other records (beginning in 1813) for this church. Includes records for slaves. Microfiche of similar records for other Charleston churches are listed in the bibliography to which this list is a supplement.

Sheriff, G. Anne. *Black History in Pickens District, South Carolina.* Easley, S.C.: Forest Acres Elementary School, 1991.

Vernon, Amelia Wallace. *African Americans at Mars Bluff, South Carolina.* Baton Rouge, La.: Louisiana State University Press, 1993.

Tennessee

Bowden, Martha Burden. *Mountain of Dreams.* Sevierville, Tenn.: Nandel Publishing, 1988. Applicable to the Dockery and Burden families in Sevier County.

Brasfield, Curtis. "'To my daughter and the heirs of her boy': Slave Passages as Illustrated by the Latham Smithwick Family." *National Genealogical Society Quarterly* 81, no. 4 (December 1993).

Texas

Devereaux, Linda Ericson. *Nacogdoches County, Texas: The Black Marriages 1866–1874.* Nacogdoches, Tex.:, 1991.

Gawalt, Gerard W. "Jefferson's Slaves: Crop accounts at Monticello, 1805–1808." *Journal of the AAHGS* 13, nos. 1 & 2 (Spring/Fall 1994).

Prather, Patricia Smith. *From Slave to Statesman: The Legacy of Joshua Houston, Servant to Sam Houston.* Denton, Tex.: University of North Texas Press, 1993. Includes both biographical and family information.

Virginia

Ibrahim, Karen King. *Fauquier County, Virginia Register of Free Negroes, 1817–1865.* Midland, Va.: Afro-American Association of Fauquier County, 1993.

King, Helen H., et al. *Historic Notes on Isle of Wight County.* Isle of Wight, Va.: Isle of Wight County Board of Supervisors, 1993. This is especially noteworthy from the standpoint of African-American research for the antebellum free black listings contained in the appendixes.

McLeroy, Sherrie. *Strangers in Their Midst: The Free Black Population of Amnerst County, Virginia.* Bowie, Md.: Heritage Books, 1993.

Smith, Gloria. *Black Americans at Mount Vernon: Genealogy Techniques for Slave Group Research.* Tucson, Ariz.: G. L. Smith, 1984.

Books

BASIC GENEALOGY RESEARCH

Abajian, James de T. *Blacks in Selected Newspapers, Censuses, and Other Sources: An Index to Names and Subjects.* 3 vols. Detroit: Gale, 1977. (First Supplement. 2 vols. Detroit: Gale, 1985.)

Barfield Calhoun, Louise. *History of Harris County, Georgia 1827–1961.* Columbus, Ga.: Cherith Creek Designs, 1991.

Bently, Elizabeth Petty. *The Genealogist's Address Book.* Baltimore, Md.: Genealogical Publishing, 1991.

Berlin, Ira. *Slaves Without Masters: The Free Negro in the Ante-Bellum South.* New York: Oxford University Press, 1981. (Reprint of the 1974 edition by Pantheon Books.)

Black Studies: A Select Catalog of National Archives. Washington, D.C.: National Archives Microfilm Publications, 1984.

Blockson, Charles L., and Ron Fry. *Black Genealogy.* Englewood Cliffs, N.J.: Prentice-Hall, 1977.

Cerny, Johni, and Arlene Eakle, eds. *The Source.* Salt Lake City: Ancestry Publishing, 1985.

Croom, Emily Anne. *The Genealogist's Companion and Sourcebook.* Cincinnati, Ohio: Betterway Books, 1994.

————. *Unpuzzling Your Past: A Basic Guide to Genealogy.* Cincinnati, Ohio: Betterway Books, 1989.

Curry, Leonard P. *The Free Blacks in Urban America—1850: The Shadow of the Dream*. Chicago: University of Chicago Press, 1981.

Eicholz, Alice, ed. *Ancestry's Red Book: American State, County and Town Sources*. Salt Lake City: Ancestry Publishing, 1989.

Ferraro, Eugene. *How to Obtain Birth, Death, Marriage, Divorce and Adoption Papers*. Santa Ana, Calif.: Marathon Press International, 1989.

Fletcher, William. *Recording Your Family History: A Guide to Preserving Oral History Using Audio and Video Tape*. Berkeley, Calif.: Ten Speed Press, 1989.

Goode, Kenneth G. *California Black Pioneers: A Brief Historical Survey*. Santa Barbara, Calif.: McNally and Loftin, 1974.

Greenwood, Val D. *The Researcher's Guide to American Genealogy*. Baltimore, Md.: Genealogical Publishing, 1973.

Hoopes, James. *Oral History: An Introduction for Students*. Chapel Hill, N.C.: University of North Carolina Press, 1979.

Journal of the Afro-American Historical and Genealogical Society. Bi-Annual, Washington, D.C.

Kemp, Thomas. *Vital Records Handbook*. Baltimore: Genealogical Publishing, 1988.

Kirkham, E. Kay. *Simplified Genealogy for Americans*. Salt Lake City: Deseret Book Co., 1968.

Logan, Rayford W., and Michael R. Winston. *Dictionary of American Negro Biography*. New York: W. W. Norton, 1982.

McLagan, Elizabeth. *A Peculiar Paradise: A History of Blacks in Oregon, 1788–1940*. Portland, Oreg.: Georgian Press, 1980.

National Union Catalogue of Manuscript Collections, 1959. Library of Congress, Washington, D.C.

Newman, *Debra L. List of Free Black Heads of Families in the First Census of the United States 1790*. Washington, D.C.: National Archives, 1973.

News Journals of The Patricia Liddell Researchers. Chicago: Patricia Liddell Researchers, 1993. (Available from the Vivian G. Harsh Research Collection, Woodson Regional Library, Chicago.

Organization Index to Pension Files of Veterans Who Served Between 1861 and 1900. (Buffalo soldiers and U.S. cavalry.)

Patricia Liddell Researchers Funeral Program Collection. Chicago: Patricia Liddell Researchers, YEAR. (Funeral programs of individuals mostly east of the Mississippi River. Available from the Vivian G. Harsh Research Collection, Woodson Regional Library, Chicago.)

Patricia Liddell Researchers High School Yearbook Collection. Chicago: Patricia Liddell Researchers, 1995. (Available from the Vivian G. Harsh Research Collection, Woodson Regional Library, Chicago.)

Rawick, George P., ed. *The American Slave: A Composite Autobiography.* 19 vols. Westport, Conn.: Greenwood Publishing, 1972. (Contributions in Afro-American studies, no. 11.)

Records of Black Americans: A Guide to Genealogical Research in the National Archives. Washington, D.C.: National Archives and Records Services, 1982.

Rose, James, and Alice Eichholz. *Black Genesis.* Detroit: Gale, 1978. (Out of print, available in libraries only.)

Schubert, Frank H. *On the Trail of the Buffalo Soldier: Biographies of African Americans in the U.S. Army, 1866–1917.* Wilmington, Del.: Scholarly Resources, 1994.

Scott, Jean Sampson. *Beginning an Afro-American Genealogical Pursuit.* New York: Express Printers, 1985.

Slave Narratives.

This series is based on a compilation of narratives by ex-slaves made by the Works Progress Administration (WPA) in the 1930s. It is supplemented by a similar, but smaller project undertaken by

Fisk University in the late 1920s. Bibliographies included. The complete series is as follows:

Volume 1: *From Sundown to Sunup: The Making of a Black Community*

Volumes 2–3: *South Carolina Narratives*

Volumes 4–5: *Texas Narratives*

Volume 6: *Alabama and Indiana Narratives*

Volume 7: *Oklahoma and Mississippi Narratives*

Volumes 8–10: *Arkansas Narratives, Parts 1–6*

Volume 11: *Arkansas Narratives, Part 7 and Missouri Narratives*

Volumes 12–13: *Georgia Narratives*

Volumes 14–15: *North Carolina Narratives*

Volume 16: *Kansas, Kentucky, Maryland, Ohio, Virginia and Tennessee Narratives*

Volume 17: *Florida Narratives*

Volume 18: *Unwritten History of Slavery*

Volume 19: *God Struck Me Dead* (Nashville, Tenn.: Fisk University.)

Stampp, Kenneth M., ed. *Records of Ante-Bellum Southern Plantations from the Revolution through the Civil War.* Frederick, Md.: University Publications of America, 1985.

Streets, David H. *Slave Genealogy: A Research Guide with Case Studies.* Bowie, Md.: Heritage Books, 1986.

Thorndale, William, and William Dollarhide. *Map Guide to the U.S. Census, 1790–1930.* Baltimore: Genealogical Publishing, 1987.

Walker, James Dent. *Black Genealogy: How to Begin.* Athens, Ga.: University of Georgia, 1977.

Walls, William J. *The African Methodist Episcopal Zion Church: Reality of the Black Church.* Charlotte, N.C.: A. M. E. Zion, 1974.

Walton–Raji, Angela Y. *Black Indian Genealogy Research.* Bowie, Md.: Heritage Books, 1993.

Wayman, Alexander W. *Cyclopaedia of African Methodism.* Baltimore: Methodist Episcopal Book Depository, 1882.

Westin, Jeanne Eddy. *Finding Your Roots: How Every American Can Trace His Ancestors at Home and Abroad.* New York: St. Martin's Press, 1977.

Who's Who of the Colored Race: A General Biographical Dictionary of Men and Women of African Descent. Vol. 1, 1915. Detroit: Gale, 1976.

Woodson, Carter G. *Free Negro Heads of Families in the United States in 1830.* Washington, D.C.: Association for the Study of African-American Life and History, 1925.

———. *Free Negro Owners of Slaves in the United States in 1830 Together With Absentee Ownership of Slaves in the United States in 1830.* Westport, Conn.: Negro Universities Press, 1968. (Reprint of 1924 original.)

HISTORICAL BACKGROUND INFORMATION

It is impractical to include a complete list of all the books written on African-American history. The list would probably be the size of an encyclopedia. Therefore, this section of the bibliography concentrates on books and periodicals that can best support your genealogy research. Some of these publications are no longer in print and can only be found through libraries or used book stores.

Boyd, Herb. *Down the Glory Road: Contributions of African-Americans in United States History and Culture.* New York: Avon Books, 1995.

Catterall, Helen Honor. *Judicial Cases Concerning American Slavery and the Negro.* 5 vols. New York: Negro Universities Press, 1968.

Davidson, Basil. *The African Slave Trade*. Back Bay Books, 1980.

Frazier, Franklin E., and Eric C. Lincoln. *The Negro Church in America/The Black Church Since Frazier*. New York: Schocken Books, 1974.

Gutman, Herbert G. *The Black Family in Slavery and Freedom, 1750–1925*. New York: Pantheon, 1976.

Higginson, Thomas Wentworth. *Army Life in a Black Regiment*. New York: W. W. Norton, 1984. (Originally published in 1869.)

Johnson, Daniel M., and Rex R. Campbell. *Black Migration in America, A Social Demographic History*. Durham, N.C.: Duke University Press, 1981.

Leckie, William H. *The Buffalo Soldiers: A Narrative of the Northwest Territory*. Detroit: Blaine Ethridge Books, 1981.

Quarles, Benjamin. *The Negro in the Civil War*. New York: Da Capo Press, 1989.

Travis, Dempsey J. *The Autobiography of Black Chicago*. Chicago: Urban Research Institute, 1981.

Wiley, Bell Irvin. *Southern Negroes 1861–1865*. Baton Rouge: Louisiana State University Press, 1974.

African-American Genealogy Memoirs

Alexander, Adele Logan. *Ambiguous Lives: Free Women of Color in Rural Georgia, 1789–1879*. Fayetteville, Ark.: University of Arkansas Press, 1991.

Archer, Chamber, Jr. *Growing Up Black in Rural Mississippi*. New York: Walker, 1992.

Billingsley, Andrew. *Climbing Jacob's Ladder: The Enduring Legacy of African-American Families*. New York: Simon and Schuster, 1992.

Comer, James. *Maggie's American Dream: The Life and Times of a Black Family.* New York: Plume Books, 1989.

Gates, Henry Louis, Jr. *Colored People, a Memoir.* New York: Vintage Books, 1995.

Haizlip, Shirlee Taylor. *The Sweeter the Juice.* New York: Simon and Schuster, 1994.

Ione, Carol. *Pride of Family: Four Generations of American Women of Color.* New York: Summit Books, 1991.

Khanga, Yelena, and Susan Jacoby. *Soul to Soul: The Story of a Black Russian American Family 1865–1992.* New York: W. W. Norton, 1992.

McLaurin, Melton A. *Celia, A Slave.* New York: Avon Books, 1993.

Taulbert, Clifton L. *When We Were Colored.* New York: Penguin Books, 1995.

REFERENCES FOR DATING EARLY PHOTOGRAPHS

Coar, Valencia Hollins. *A Century of Black Photographers, 1840–1960.* Providence, Rhode Island: Museum of Art, Rhode Island School of Design, 1983.

Crawford, William. *The Keepers of Light: A History and Working Guide to Early Photographic Processes.* Dobbs Ferry, N.Y.: Morgan and Morgan, 1979.

Morgan, Hal, and Andreas Brown. *Prairie Fires and Paper Moons: The American Photographic Postcard: 1900–1920.* Boston: David R. Godine, 1981.

Source: Chicago Historical Society, Department of Prints and Photographs.

Taft, Robert. *Photography and the American Scene: A Social History.* New York: Macmillan, 1938. Reprinted by Dover Publications, 1964.

Welling, William. *Collector's Guide to Nineteenth Century Photographs*. New York: Collier Books, 1976.

————. *Photography in America: The Formative Years, 1839–1900*. New York: Thomas J. Crowell Company, 1978.

Willis-Thomas, Deborah. *Black Photographers, 1840–1940: An Illustrated Bio-Bibliography*. New York: Garland Press, 1985.

COMPUTERS AND THE INTERNET

Eastman, Richard. *Your Roots: Total Genealogy Planning on Your Computer*. Emeryville, Calif.: Ziff Davis Press, 1995. Includes a CD-ROM loaded with information.

Hoffman, Allan. *50 Fun Ways to the Internet: How to Sign On, Navigate and Explore the "Net" Without Getting Lost in Cyberspace*. Careers Press, 1995.

Levine, John R., Carol Baroud, and Margaret Levine Young. *The Internet for Dummies*. 3d ed. IDG Books, Foster City, Calif.: 1995.

MaranGraphics Design Team. *Internet and World Wide Web Simplified: The 3D Visual Approach*. IDG Books, Foster City, Calif.: 1995.

Miser, Brad, Marta Partington, and Brian Gill. *Get on the Internet in 5 Minutes*. Hayden Books, 1994.

AFRICAN-AMERICAN GENEALOGY MICROFILM SOURCES

Most microfilm can be found at the National Archives in Washington, D.C., and at the regional branch archives. Also check state archives and various libraries.

Microfilm can also be ordered through the National Archives, Black Studies, Catalog of Microfilm Publications. To request a catalog write to:

Publication Sales Branch (NEPS)
National Archives
Washington, D.C. 20408

This catalog may also be available at a government bookstore in your city.

BUREAU OF REFUGEES, FREEDMEN, AND ABANDONED LANDS

RECORDS OF THE ASSISTANT COMMISSIONER FOR THE FOLLOWING STATES. Alabama, Arkansas, Georgia, Mississippi, North Carolina, Tennessee, Texas, and Virginia.

RECORDS OF THE EDUCATION DIVISION, 1865–71. Washington, D.C.: National Archives and Records Service, thirty-five reels, 35mm microfilm.

REGISTERS AND LETTERS RECEIVED BY THE COMMISSIONER, 1865–72. Washington, D.C.: National Archives and Records Service, seventy-four reels, 35mm microfilm.

Census Records

MISSISSIPPI MARRIAGES (SELECTED). Microfilm copies are available for the following cities and years: Alcorn, 1866–1921; Bolivar, 1866–1916; Clarke, 1865–1919; George, 1910–21; Franklin, 1871–1928; Lauderdale, 1870–1916. Available in many genealogical research collections.

MORTALITY SCHEDULES. Records for following states and years: Alabama, 1850; Georgia, 1850–80; Louisiana, 1850–80; Texas, 1850–80. Available in several genealogical research collections.

SLAVE CENSUSES FOR THE SOUTHERN STATES: 1850–60. Available at the National Archives and in several genealogical research collections throughout the United States.

Freedmen's Bureau

RECORDS RELATING TO DESTITUTE FREEDMEN AND REFUGEES. A series of narrative reports that describe the financial and logistical plans of local boards to meet the needs of destitute freedmen living within their jurisdiction. Lists of destitute freedmen are arranged by district. Monthly lists of unemployed freedmen from March 1866 to December 1869 are arranged chronologically. Available on microfilm from the National Archives.

RECORDS RELATING TO MURDERS AND OUTRAGES. A descriptive list of reports and outrages committed on freedmen in 1868 resulting from employment discharges, from exercising the right to vote, and from participating in political organizations. Includes statements by freedmen who were victims of abuses in

Richmond, Virginia, during June 1865. These records are part of the Freedmen's Bureau records available at the National Archives.

FREEDMEN'S SAVINGS AND TRUST COMPANY

INDEXES TO DEPOSIT LEDGERS IN VARIOUS BRANCHES, 1865–74.
Available on microfilm from the National Archives and Records Service in Washington, D.C.

Indexes are available for the following *states*.

Alabama	Kentucky	North Carolina
Arkansas	Louisiana	Pennsylvania
District of Columbia	Maryland	South Carolina
Florida	Mississippi	Tennessee
Georgia	Missouri	Virginia

Records available from the following *cities*.

Augusta, Georgia	New Bern, North Carolina
Baltimore, Maryland	New Orleans, Louisiana
Beaufort, South Carolina	Norfolk, Virginia
Charleston, South Carolina	Philadelphia, Pennsylvania
Huntsville, Alabama	Raleigh, North Carolina
Jacksonville, Florida/	Richmond, Virginia
all of Arkansas	Savannah, Georgia
Lexington, Kentucky/	Shreveport, Louisiana
all of Massachusetts	St. Louis, Missouri
Little Rock, Arkansas	Tallahassee, Florida
Louisville, Kentucky	Vicksburg, Mississippi
Memphis, Tennessee	Washington, D.C.
Nashville, Tennessee	Wilmington, Delaware
Natchez, Mississippi	

SIGNATURE BOOKS. Names from the following cities.

Atlanta, Georgia
Augusta, Georgia
Baltimore, Maryland
Charleston, South Carolina
Columbus, Ohio
Huntsville, Alabama
Lexington, Kentucky/
  Massachusetts/Little Rock,
  Arkansas
Louisville, Kentucky
Lynchburg, Virginia
Memphis, Tennessee
Nashville, Tennessee

Natchez, Mississippi
New Bern, North Carolina
New Orleans, Louisiana
Norfolk, Virginia
Philadelphia, Pennsylvania
Raleigh, North Carolina
Savannah, Georgia
Shreveport, Louisiana
St. Louis, Missouri
Tallahassee, Florida
Washington, D.C.
Wilmington, Delaware

Available from the National Archives, Washington, D.C., and other library genealogical collections throughout the United States.

INDIAN-RELATED RECORDS

BUREAU OF INDIAN AFFAIRS—ENROLLMENT CARDS OF THE FIVE CIVILIZED TRIBES: 1898-1914. Enrollment cards, sometimes called census cards, recorded such information as the applicant's name, roll number, age, sex, degree of Indian blood, relationship to the head of the family group, and death. Cards also included information on freedmen (former black slaves of Indians, later freed and admitted to tribal citizenship). Freedmen records for the following tribes are included: Cherokee, Choctaw, Creek, Chickasaw, and Seminole. Available on microfilm at the National Archives and some genealogical research collections.

MILITARY RECORDS

CONGRESSIONAL MEDAL OF HONOR WINNERS FROM THE CIVIL WAR TO THE SPANISH AMERICAN WAR. Includes listing of Medal of Honor winners for both the Army and Navy and enlisted men and officers. Also includes listing of the Seminole-Negro Indian scouts who served with the U.S. Army and were awarded the Congressional Medal of Honor. Washington, D.C.: National Archives and Records Service, four reels.

INDEX TO THE COMPILED SERVICE RECORDS FOR UNITED STATES COLORED TROOPS. Washington, D.C.: National Archives and Records Service, microfilm 713.

LETTERS SENT BY THE DEPARTMENT OF TEXAS, THE DISTRICT OF TEXAS, AND THE 5TH MILITARY DISTRICT: 1856–58 AND 1865–70. Includes records on the 38th, 41st, 24th, and 25th Infantry Regiments, created as black regiments, which were stationed in Texas. All four of these black regiments served in campaigns against the Indians in the Southwest. Washington, D.C.: National Archives and Records Service, three rolls.

NAVAL RECORDS COLLECTION: CORRESPONDENCE OF THE SECRETARY OF THE NAVY RELATING TO AFRICAN COLONIZATION, 1819–1844. The correspondence consists mainly of copies of letters sent by the Secretary of the Navy to agents of the United States stationed on the northwest coast of Africa for the purpose of receiving blacks freed by the capture of slave ships. Washington, D.C.: National Archives and Records Service, two microfilm reels.

NEGROES IN THE MILITARY OF THE UNITED STATES: 1639–1866. Washington, D.C.: National Archives and Records Service. Compilation of official records, state papers, and historical extracts relating to the service of blacks in the United States military.

RETURNS FROM REGULAR ARMY CAVALRY REGIMENTS: 1833–1916. The 9th and 10th Cavalry were formed right after the Civil War. Indians named them buffalo soldiers. The enlisted men were blacks, and the officers were white. Returns report the strength of each regiment in total number of men present, absent or sick. A specific accounting of men by name is given. Available at the National Archives and Records Service.

RETURNS FROM REGULAR ARMY INFANTRY REGIMENTS: JUNE 1821–DECEMBER 1916. Returns report the strength of each regiment in total number of men present, absent or sick. A specific accounting of men by name is given. Includes records on the 38th, 31st, 24th, and 25th Black Infantry Regiments. Washington, D.C.: National Archives and Records Service, reels 245–61 and 293–96.

SELECTED DOCUMENTS RELATING TO BLACKS NOMINATED FOR APPOINTMENT TO THE U.S. MILITARY ACADEMY DURING THE NINETEENTH CENTURY: 1870–87. Washington, D.C.: National Archives and Records Service, twenty-one reels, 35mm microfilm.

MISCELLANEOUS

CARTER G. WOODSON COLLECTION OF NEGRO PAPERS AND RELATED DOCUMENTS: 1803–1936. Correspondence, diaries, addresses, legal documents, newspaper clippings, and other papers related to Negro history, slavery, employment opportunities, business, state and local politics, and the African Methodist Episcopal (A.M.E.) Church. Washington, D.C.: Library of Congress.

NEGRO NEWSPAPERS ON MISCELLANEOUS REELS. Microfilmed by Library of Congress, Washington, D.C., for the Committee on Negro Studies of the American Council of Learning Societies, 1947. Newspapers from the forty-eight contiguous states dating from 1865.

PLANTATION LIFE

RECORDS OF ANTEBELLUM SOUTHERN PLANTATIONS. This is a series of records from a wide variety of sources. It is published by University Publications of America (Bethesda, Maryland). The collection can be found in several libraries with genealogical collections throughout the United States. See the listing of libraries in this appendix.

This collection can provide insight into plantation life, slave purchases and sales, and the plantation owner's viewpoint on his day-to-day life. If you're researching large southern plantations, they may be of interest or value in tracing your ancestry.

SERIES A: SELECTIONS FROM THE SOUTH CAROLINA LIBRARY: PART 1. Features the extensive papers of James Henry Hammond, a wealthy plantation owner. Also, Series A: Selections from the South Carolina Library: Part 2. Includes plantation owners from every region of South Carolina, from rice plantations to coastal lowlands to cotton plantations.

SERIES B: SELECTIONS FROM THE SOUTH CAROLINA HISTORICAL SOCIETY. Papers of families and individuals from South Carolina's low country, St. John's Parish of Charleston District, Black Oak Agricultural Society, Alonzo White's auction books, and Reverend Alexander Glennie's diary.

SERIES C, PARTS 1 AND 2: SELECTIONS FROM THE LIBRARY OF CONGRESS. Records and correspondence of several Virginia planters, including William B. Randolph, Hill Carter, and the Bruce Family.

SERIES D: SELECTIONS FROM THE MARYLAND HISTORICAL SOCIETY. Materials from smaller plantations and the diary of Martha Foreman.

SERIES E, PARTS 1–3. Contains the Watson family papers and from every region of Old Dominion; diary and letterbooks of "King"

Carter; papers of the Berkeley family; diary of Louisa H. A. Minor and her family records; and Southern border counties' collections.

SERIES F, PARTS 1–3: SELECTIONS FROM DUKE UNIVERSITY LIBRARY. Records from the Old Southwest, Henry Watson and Clement Claiborne Clay papers of Alabama; papers of John Knight and Duncan McLaurin of Mississippi; materials from low-country plantations of absentee "rice Barons"; and documentation on interstate slave trade.

SLAVERY

AMERICAN ANTI-SLAVERY SOCIETY: ANNUAL REPORTS, NUMBERS 1–27. Westport, Conn.: Greenwood Press. Includes annual speeches, anniversary meetings, roll of delegates, officers and minutes. Available in various genealogical library research collections.

SLAVERY TRACTS AND PAMPHLETS FROM THE WEST INDIA COMMITTEE COLLECTION. London: World Microfilm Publications. A collection of pamphlets on the sugar trade and slave labor. Available in various genealogical library research collections.

Index